Defining the Republic

Defining the Republic

Early Conflicts over the Constitution

William J. Nichols

LEXINGTON BOOKS
Lanham • Boulder • New York • London

Published by Lexington Books
An imprint of The Rowman & Littlefield Publishing Group, Inc.
4501 Forbes Boulevard, Suite 200, Lanham, Maryland 20706
www.rowman.com

86-90 Paul Street, London EC2A 4NE

British Library Cataloguing in Publication Information Available

Library of Congress Cataloging-in-Publication Data Available

ISBN: 978-1-7936-5536-3 (cloth : alk. paper)
ISBN: 978-1-7936-5537-0 (electronic)

Contents

Introduction

This book is entitled *Defining the Republic: Early Conflicts over the Constitution* because it is a comparison of the definitions of what specifically the newly founded republic of the United States should be like between the views of Alexander Hamilton and James Madison. I have chosen to compare these two Founders because they could agree on the form of government they wanted for the United States, namely the Constitution, but once they attained their goal, they became bitter political enemies since they could not agree on how to implement the Constitution they had both worked so hard to obtain. That is, they had conflicting definitions of, and expectations for, what the republic of the United States would be like.

Hamilton and Madison were not the only two Founders with conflicting definitions of what the United States should be. Anyone who looks at the conflict over ratification of the Constitution will see a wide variety of visions. Also, the political conflicts beginning in the 1790s only add more material showing the range of disagreement among the Founders.

One individual who specifically mentioned the problem of defining a republic was John Adams. In one letter he wrote Mercy Warren about his objections to her history of the American Revolution, he said:

> The first appearance of a national stipulation in favor of Republican government was in the Constitution of the United States, in which a Republican constitution was guaranteed to the several States. It may perhaps be a sufficient recommendation of this article to say that it was introduced by Mr. Charles Pinckney, of South Carolina; and he ought to have the glory of it. But I confess I never understood of, and I believe no other man ever did, or ever will.[1]

One problem with the word "republic," as Adams pointed out, is it has been given so many definitions throughout history. Adams stated a republic is a government of "more than one," but goes on to argue this is almost no definition at all. "A Republican government is a government of more than one.

The word Republic has been used, it is true, by learned men, to signify every actual and every possible government among men—that of Constantinople as well as that of Geneva."[2]

For Adams, the distinction then is between republics which are free and those which are not free.

> The most accurate distinction, then, has been between free republics and republics which are not free. It is not even said in our Constitution that the people shall be guaranteed a free and republican government. The word is so loose and indefinite that successive predominant factions will put glosses and constructions on it as different as light and darkness; and if ever there should be a civil war, which Heaven forbid, the conquering General in all his triumph may establish a military despotism, and yet call it a constitutional republic, as Napoleon has already set him the example. The only effect of it that I could ever see is to deceive the people; and this practice my heart abhors, my head disapproves, and my tongue and my pen have ever avoided. I am no Pharisee, Jesuit, or Machiavellian.[3]

Adams points out just how "loose and indefinite" the word republic is, how many different types of government have been identified as republics, and the danger that follows from relying on such an ill-defined word to describe and understand just what form of government the United States exists under. It is that difficulty in defining the word republic I want to further explore through my comparison of Hamilton and Madison.

Now, Hamilton and Madison did not see their disagreements as a matter of conflicting definitions of "republic," or indeed any other word. They simply wanted different things for the United States. The reason I argue for taking the approach I advocate in comparing their conflicting visions is that by focusing on a word central to both (after all, both considered themselves republicans), one gains a theme around which to organize such a comparison. This means it can also be used for other Founders, and later individuals as well.

Examination of the ideas of the Founders is important because of the influence they had on later generations down to today. All sorts of individuals, from all sorts of ideological perspectives, call upon the Founders in support of their policy goals. However, the Founders were not the coherent group, with coherent sets of ideas and political principles, that many would like them to be. So it is rather to their differences and to their conflicts that we must look to fully understand their influence. In so doing we can not only more completely understand them, but ourselves as well.

As I mentioned above, there is no one conclusive definition of the word "republic," and so what it means for the United States to be a republic has been a source of constant debate throughout its history. The differences Hamilton and Madison had will help highlight that debate, as both were pivotal figures in the early history of the United States, and their influence has continued to this day.

Also, in essence, what divided Hamilton and Madison was a sense of what was truly "American." Since each perceived his ideas and preferences regarding the United States to be the best, indeed the *only*, ideas about what the United States should be, thus the other's ideas "had" to be un-American. This idea of being "un-American" has been discussed in detail by Brian Steele. He argues it is with Thomas Jefferson that we can find the origins of Americans thinking of other Americans as not truly, genuinely American, indeed as "un-American."

> Americans would recognize each other—not by language and appearance, not by ethnicity or religion—but by their common adherence to what Jefferson later called the "principles of '76." Americans had cast off the "unfeeling brethren" to join in a union of what Jefferson called in his First Inaugural "brethren of the same principle."[4]

So, was either Hamilton or Madison "un-American?" I argue neither was. Both were clearly loyal, passionate Americans, dedicated to the Revolutionary ideals of liberty. That they emphasized different aspects of those Revolutionary ideals does not make either any less or more a true American than the other. One can clearly see that Hamilton and Madison were far from the only leading figures of the early Republic who had contrasting ideas. One need only look at the break in friendship between John Adams and Thomas Jefferson to see an example of that.

Akhil Reed Amar also argues, as I do, that Hamilton and Madison agreed on the basics, but differed on how those basics were to be implemented. Also, he argues that Hamilton and Madison were in different political situations and thus had to respond to different influences and constraints.

> At first, the first man in the first branch in the Constitution's first years was a strong supporter of America's First Man and that First Man's first cabinet minister. But over time James Madison came to oppose George Washington and Alexander Hamilton, and indeed to disavow his own previous positions. Ironically, Madison, Washington, and Hamilton were yanked in different directions by divergent political incentives and conversational structures implicit in the very Constitution they themselves had jointly created and, initially, jointly consolidated.
>
> Even as these titans tugged against each other—or, to be more precise, even as Madison tugged against the other two—the three men continued to share a common constitutional grammar and culture, as did the broader American society surrounding them. Early Americans generally played by the same basic ground rules of interpretation, placing the Constitution itself on a deservedly

> high pedestal and attending closely to the document's text, structure, purpose, and enactment history. On many but not all issues, Hamilton simply played the interpretive game better. That is, his arguments meshed more tightly with the Constitution's letter and spirit, and with what he and other Federalists had said and written in explaining and selling the document to the American people in the ratification process. When Hamilton's interpretive arguments were strong, as they often were, Washington and America generally sided with him. But in certain constitutional contests where Madison and his allies played the interpretive game better—where their arguments excelled on the merits, especially where basic rights were at stake—America would dramatically side with them, as we shall see in the next chapter. In a system ultimately driven by common folk with only limited constitutional knowledge, vision, and attention span, America not only somehow managed to pick truly great men and put them in the right slots at the right time, but also somehow managed to outperform them all in sensibly applying the Constitution's letter and spirit.[5]

Those individuals we call the Founders disagreed about a wide range of issues, but what I point to is the persistence of their ways of thinking even to this day. Most Americans favor a strong military establishment, and in so doing are perpetuating the preferences of Federalists such as Hamilton. On the other hand, the strong emphasis on the importance of individual rights, such as freedom of religion, shows the persistence of the ideas of the Democratic-Republicans such as Madison.

Yes, the Federalists were done after 1800, but their ideas did not go away. One can see the ways in which at least some of their ideas were continued by the more national-oriented Democratic-Republicans, then the National Republicans, Whigs, the later Republican Party especially during its first few decades of existence, and even in Franklin Delano Roosevelt's Democratic Party New Deal.

I argue it is this perception of political differences as indicative of un-Americanness that is one cause of the faulty perception of the American people as a whole being just as widely divided on political issues as the elites were and are. Morris Fiorina has argued persuasively that, while political elites are passionately divided on political issues, as Hamilton and Madison were, the American people are not anywhere near as divided.

> This short book advances a contrary thesis: the sentiments expressed in the previously quoted pronouncements of scholars, journalists, and politicos range from simple exaggeration to sheer nonsense. Such assertions both reflect and contribute to a widespread mythology about contemporary American politics. The simple truth is that there is no culture war in the United States—no battle for the soul of America rages, at least none that most Americans are aware of. Certainly, one can find a few faux-warriors who engage in noisy skirmishes.

> Many of the activists in the political parties and the various cause groups do, in fact, hate each other and regard themselves as combatants in a war. But their hatreds and battles are not shared by the great mass of the American people—certainly nowhere near the "80–90 percent of the country"—who are for the most part moderate in their views and tolerant in their manner. Most Americans are somewhat like the unfortunate citizens of some third-world countries who try to stay out of the crossfire while left-wing guerrillas and right-wing death squads shoot at each other.[6]

From my studies of Hamilton and Madison, presently below, one can see the passionate response each had to the realization that their views on policy were not the same. I argue, adding to Fiorina's thesis, that it is during times of transition that elites become far more divided than during times of relative tranquility. This occurred in the 1790s, has reoccurred several times over the history of the United States, and most certainly is the case today.

NOTES

1. John Adams and Mercy Warren, *Correspondence Between John Adams and Mercy Warren* (New York: Arno Press, 1972), 352–353.
2. Ibid, 353.
3. Ibid, 353.
4. Brian Steele, "Inventing Un-American," *Journal of American Studies* 47, no. 4 (November 2013): 886.
5. Akhil Reed Amar, *The Words That Made Us: America's Constitutional Conversation, 1760–1840* (New York: Basic Books, 2021), 349–350.
6. Morris P. Fiorina, with Samuel J. Abrams and Jeremy C. Pope, *Culture War? The Myth of a Polarized America*, Third Edition (Boston: Longman, 2011), 8.

Chapter One

Definitions of a Republic from Other Authors

Since this book is an examination of the idea of a republic according to the preferences of Alexander Hamilton and James Madison, I will dedicate this chapter to a discussion of the background to the idea of a republic throughout history. In so doing, my approach is heavily influenced by J.G.A. Pocock's *The Machiavellian Moment*, although I will include some figures he does not in my presentation. Regardless of whether they are all strictly within the historical development of republican thought as it is currently understood, I argue the individuals I include are worth discussing because Hamilton and Madison did not concern themselves with the intellectual categories that we later academics use. Their thought on what constituted "proper" republicanism drew on a wider range of influences.

As Pocock argues, though, the primary source for what we now identify as republican thought, with its emphasis on a mixed constitution, is Polybius and his *The Histories*.

> The sixth book of Polybius' *Histories*, though it did not become available in a language other than Greek until the second decade of the sixteenth century, exercised so great an influence on Renaissance ideas about politics in time that it may be considered here as indicative of that age's fundamental conceptual problems.[1]

As is well known, Polybius borrowed the idea for a mixed constitution from Aristotle, but further elaborated on and expanded Aristotle's ideas. The whole point of positing a mixture of different political systems was stability, at least one which would conceivably last longer than any of the stages through which Polybius argues societies moved as a matter of regular history.

> In the natural, spontaneous course of events, the first system to arise is monarchy, and this is followed by kingship, but it takes the deliberate correction of

> the defects of monarchy for it to develop into kingship. Kingship changes into its congenital vice—that is, into tyranny—and then it is the turn of aristocracy, after the dissolution of tyranny. Aristocracy necessarily degenerates into oligarchy, and when the general populace get impassioned enough to seek redress for the crimes committed by their leaders, democracy is born. And in due course of time, once democracy turns to violating and breaking the law, mob-rule arises and completes the series.[2]

Polybius's cure for this endless cycle is once again the mixture of all three types of government at its best, kingship, aristocracy, and democracy, specifically exemplified by the Roman republic. The three components, or building blocks, as Polybius called them, were the consuls, which provided the kingship element, the senate, which provided the aristocratic element, and the people, which provided the democratic element. "To a considerable extent, then, each of the three components of the Roman constitution can harm or help the other two. This enables the whole made up of all three parts to respond appropriately to every situation that arises, and that is what makes it the best conceivable system of government."[3]

I will follow a historical approach to discussing the other authors who followed in Polybius's footsteps, so the next individual I have included is Cicero, the Roman senator. He also discussed the possible types of government as including monarchy, aristocracy, and democracy.

> When, therefore, the supreme power is in the hands of one man, we call that man a king and that form of government a monarchy. When it is in the hands of certain selected persons, the state is said to be ruled by the will of an aristocracy. And a state is democratic—for that is the term used—when all authority is in the hands of the people themselves. Any one of these three forms of government, while not, of course, perfect nor in my judgment the best, is nevertheless a possible form of government, if the bond holds which originally united its members in the social order of the commonwealth; and one may be better than another.[4]

Cicero does not posit the same cycle of governments as Polybius, merely listing the options he sees as possible. However, he does argue there is in fact a kind of government which is superior to any of these three, and here we see a continuation of Polybius's mixed model. "There is, accordingly, a fourth kind of commonwealth which, in my opinion, should receive the highest approval, since it is formed by the combination, in due measure, of the three forms of state which I described as original."[5]

Machiavelli, in *The Discourses on Livy*, also presents Polybius's cycle without specifically referring to him by name. Humans originally select the strongest man among them to rule, and thus begins the cycle through kingship, tyranny, aristocracy, oligarchy, democracy, anarchy, and then begin the cycle all over again. However, there is a kind of government that is better than any of these by itself.

> I say, then, that all kinds of government are defective; those three which we have qualified as good because they are too short-lived, and the three bad ones because of their inherent viciousness. Thus sagacious legislators, knowing the vices of each of these systems of government by themselves, have chosen one that should partake of all of them, judging that to be the most stable and solid. In fact, when there is combined under the same constitution a prince, a nobility, and the power of the people, then these three powers will watch and keep each other reciprocally in check.[6]

Machiavelli argues the origin of this especially worthwhile form of government comes from a gifted legislator, who sets up laws which thereafter are complied with throughout subsequent generations. For Machiavelli, one such legislator was Lycurgus, whose model of government for Sparta lasted for centuries. Even though Rome did not have any such individual legislator, though, it nevertheless developed the type of government of which Machiavelli approves.

> But let us come to Rome. Although she had no legislator like Lycurgus, who constituted her government, at her very origin, in a manner to secure her liberty for a length of time, yet the disunion which existed between the Senate and the people produced such extraordinary events, that chance did for her what the laws had failed to do. Thus, if Rome did not attain the first degree of happiness, she at least had the second. Her first institutions were doubtless defective, but they were not in conflict with the principles that might bring her to perfection.[7]

Returning to Pocock, he argues the "glue," if you will, of this preferred, mixed form of government, according to Machiavelli, is virtue. Just having the structural elements of a monarchical element, an aristocratical element, and a democratic element, are not enough. What is needed in addition is, specifically, "civic" virtue, in order for such republics to succeed.

> The republic or polity was in yet another sense a structure of virtue: it was a structure in which every citizen's ability to place the common good before his own was the precondition of every other's, so that every man's virtue saved every other's from that corruption part of whose time-dimension was *fortuna*. The republic was therefore a structure whose organizing principle was something far more complex and positive than custom.[8]

Pocock ascribes the importation of Machiavellian republican influence into England to the political conflict which led to that nation's Civil War. Instead of monarchical and feudal ideas, some allowance was held to be needed for the other sources of political power, namely the aristocracy and the people. Pocock identifies the crucial step as having been taken by Charles I's advisors.

> On 21 June 1642, with about two months to go before the formal beginnings of civil war, two of Charles I's advisors—Viscount Falkland and Sir John Colepeper—drafted, and persuaded him to issue, a document in which the King, not Parliament, took the step of declaring England a mixed government rather than a condescending monarchy. *His Majesty's Answer to the Nineteen Propositions of Both Houses of Parliament* . . . is a crucial document in English political thought, and among other things one of a series of keys which opened the door to Machiavellian analysis. In essence, it asserts that the government of England is vested in three estates, the King, the lords, and the commons, and that the health and the very survival of the system depend upon maintenance of the balance between them.[9]

While he is not included among the authors Pocock discusses, I am including Thomas Hobbes because of his undisputed place in the development of English, and thus later American, political thought. Hobbes also identifies three main types of government, monarchy, aristocracy, and democracy. However, for Hobbes, the most important goal for any form of government, is not virtue as with Machiavelli, but rather peace and security. "The difference between these three kindes of Common-wealth, consisteth not in the difference of Power; but in the difference of Convenience, or Aptitude to produce the Peace, and Security of the people; for which end they were instituted."[10]

For Hobbes, the kind of government whose end result is most clearly the peace and security of the people, is in fact monarchy. Hobbes argues that the interest of the monarch is the same as that of the country as a whole, and thus monarchy is best suited to creating the hoped-for outcomes of peace and security.

> From whence it follows, that where the publique and private interest are most closely united, there is the publique most advanced. Now, in Monarchy, the private interest is the same with the publique. The riches, power, and honour of a Monarch arise onely from the riches, strength and reputation of his Subjects. For no King can be rich, nor glorious, nor secure; whose subjects are either poore, or contemptible, or too weak through want, or dissension, to maintain a war against their enemies: Whereas in a Democracy, or Aristocracy, the publique prosperity conferres not so much to the private fortune of one that is corrupt, or ambitious, as doth many times a perfidious advice, a treacherous action, or a Civill warre.[11]

It is with James Harrington, however, who Pocock does identify as being clearly within the republican tradition, that we begin to receive even more details regarding what a republic should be like, more than just having a mixed government. For Harrington, land ownership, and also possession of weapons, is vital.

> But the tillage, bringing up a good soldiery, bringeth up a good commonwealth . . . for where the owner of the plough comes to have the sword too, he will use it in defence of his own, whence it hath happened that the people of Oceana, in proportion to their property, have always been free, and the genius of this nation hath ever had some resemblance with that of ancient Italy, which was wholly addicted unto commonwealths, and where Rome came to make the greatest account of her rustic tribes and to call her consuls from the plough.[12]

It is this ownership of land, though, which specifically provides for Harrington the means of balancing power within a commonwealth. Rather than relying solely on civic virtue, having a successful commonwealth means the otherwise weakest of the three, the people, have sufficient land to counteract the power of the other two. "And if the whole people be landlords, or hold the lands so divided among them, that no one man, or number of men, within the compass of the few or aristocracy, overbalance them, the empire *without the interposition of force* is a commonwealth."[13]

Furthermore, Harrington defines "popular government" as the best, because it best approximates what human beings can accomplish through the use of their reason.

> Mankind then must either be less just than the creature, or acknowledge also his common interest to be common right. And if reason be nothing else but interest, and the interest of mankind be the right interest, then the reason of mankind must be right reason. Now compute well, for if the interest of popular government come the nearest unto the interest of mankind, then the reason of popular government must come the nearest unto right reason.[14]

But what, exactly, kind of "popular government" did Harrington intend in *The Commonwealth of Oceana*? Not only does his ideal form of government rely on widespread land ownership, armed commoners, and a mixed government, it also specifically includes voting rights. Missing are references to a hereditary monarchy, or a hereditary aristocracy as well.

> An equal commonwealth *by that which hath been said* is a government established upon an equal agrarian, arising into the superstructures or three orders, the senate debating and proposing, the people resolving, and the magistracy executing by an equal rotation through the suffrage of the people given by the ballot.[15]

John Locke is another author who, like Thomas Hobbes, is not included among those considered by Pocock to be within the republican tradition. Nevertheless, any discussion of background influences on early Americans such as Hamilton and Madison would be incomplete without noting his contributions.

To begin, Locke of course argues that organized societies come into being through the consent of the people who constitute them, in order to better protect their "liberty and property." For Locke, there are specific goals people have in mind when they make the choice to live together rather than apart. Those goals limit the range of actions any government the people choose to create can take on its own. Moreover, the primary part of government for Locke is in fact the legislature which is the first thing created.

> THE great end of mens entering into Society, being the enjoyment of the Properties in Peace and Safety, and the great instrument and means of that being the Laws established in that Society; the *first and fundamental positive Law* of all Common-wealths, *is the establishing of the Legislative* Power; as the *first and fundamental natural law*.[16]

Not only is the form of government chosen by the people who choose to create it limited in what it can do, the people who created it can change the government itself if they so choose: "there remains still *in the People a Supream Power* to remove or *alter the Legislative*, when they find the *Legislative* act contrary to the trust reposed in them."[17]

Furthermore, the government itself can even be removed if that is felt to be necessary. "There is therefore, secondly, another way whereby *Governments are dissolved*, and that is; when the Legislative, or the Prince, either of them act contrary to their Trust."[18]

Algernon Sidney, writing, like Locke, in response to Sir Robert Filmer's *Patriarcha*, makes arguments quite similar to Locke's in regard to the origins and limited powers of government. His arguments do include the notion of "justice" in the forming of governments, though. "The liberty of one is thwarted by that of another; and whilst they are all equal, none will yield to any, otherwise than by a general consent. This is the ground of all just governments; for violence or fraud can create no right; and the same consent gives the form to them all, how much soever they differ from each other."[19]

The purpose of creating government, according to Sidney, is justice, and those who are given power under any form of government, are there to carry out justice. Justice is the good of the society, not of any one individual or group within that society.

'Tis lawful therefore for any such bodies to set up one, or a few men to govern them, or to retain the power in themselves; and he or they who are set up, having no other power but what is conferred upon them by that multitude, whether great or small, are truly by them made what they are; and by the law of their own creation, are to exercise those powers according to the proportion, and to the ends for which they were given.[20]

Sidney does give pride of place to mixed government as being the best of all possible choices. "And if I should undertake to say, there never was a good government in the world, that did not consist of the three simple species of monarchy, aristocracy and democracy, I think I might make it good."[21]

Like Locke, Sidney clearly states that governments can be changed as desired: "whilst the foundation and principle of a government remains good, the superstructures may be changed according to occasions, without any prejudice to it."[22]

Sidney's main concern is with "corruption," which, even if a government is initially set up well, can cause its decline into despotism. Corruption for Sidney is ultimately reliance on the monarch for one's income, since it is in absolute monarchies that corruption inevitably occurs.

This being the state of the matter on both sides, we may easily collect, that all governments are subject to corruption and decay; but with this difference, that absolute monarchy is by principle led unto, or rooted in it; whereas mixed or popular governments are only in a possibility of falling into it: As the first cannot subsist, unless the prevailing part of the people be corrupted; the other must certainly perish, unless they be preserved in a great measure free from vices: and I doubt whether any better reason can be given, why there have been and are more monarchies than popular governments in the world, than that nations are more easily drawn into corruption than defended from it; and I think that monarchy can be said to be natural in no other sense, than that our depraved nature is most inclined to that which is worst.[23]

This need for virtue in Sidney's thought does reveal a conflict within his argument. At one point he admits that aristocratically rooted governments are less subject to corruption than popular, or democratically rooted governments. "If it be said, that those governments in which the democratical part governs most, do more frequently err in the choice of men or of the means of preserving that purity of manners which is required for the well-being of a people, than those wherein aristocracy prevails; I confess it."[24]

However, just sentences later, he extols the virtues of democracy as the form of government most likely to be the best one possible: "and of all governments, democracy, in which every man's liberty is least restrained, because every man hath an equal part, would certainly prove to be the most just, rational and natural."[25]

Be that as it may, Sidney's goal in *Discourses Concerning Government* is to argue against absolute monarchies, because they are the most unjust possible form of government. Power comes from the people, not from divine right. Power proceeds upward from the people to their magistrates and does not descend from a divinely appointed monarch.

> I take liberty to say, that whereas there is no form appointed by God or nature, those governments only can be called just, which are established by the consent of nations. These nations may at the first set up popular or mixed governments, and without the guilt of sedition introduce them afterwards, if that which was first established prove unprofitable or hurtful to them; and those that have done so, have enjoy'd more justice in times of peace, and managed wars, when occasion requir'd, with more virtue and better success, than any absolute monarchies have done.[26]

Sidney was a martyr to other Whigs, especially the later "True Whig" writers who were so influential with the leaders of the American Revolution. His *Discourses Concerning Government* were the source of ideas which revolutionary leaders across the colonies called upon to justify their complaints regarding the actions of Parliament and King. Some passages of his need only be mentioned to show the influence of his thought. "But those who seek after truth, will easily find, that there can be no such thing in the world as the rebellion of a nation against its own magistrates, and that rebellion is not always evil."[27]

This passage also needs no further comment in regard to not only the ideas, but the actions taken, by leaders of the American Revolution.

> But tho every private man singly taken be subject to the commands of the magistrate, the whole body of the people is not so; for he is by and for the people, and the people is neither by nor for him. The obedience due to him from private men is grounded upon, and measured by the general law; and that law regarding the welfare of the people, cannot set up the interest of one or a few men against the publick. The whole body therefore of a nation cannot be tied to any other obedience than is consistent with the common good, according to their own judgment: and having never been subdued or brought to terms of peace with their magistrates, they cannot be said to revolt or rebel against them to whom they owe no more than seems good to themselves, and who are nothing of or by themselves, more than other men.[28]

Charles-Louis de Secondat, Baron de la Brede et de Montesquieu, as has been demonstrated by Donald Lutz,[29] was cited a comparable number of times as John Locke during the 1760s and 1770s (15 vs. 18), and his influence on the separation of powers debate clearly justifies his inclusion here. Montesquieu identifies a somewhat different set of possible governments than do the other authors I have thus far discussed.

> There are three kinds of government: REPUBLICAN, MONARCHICAL, and DESPOTIC. To discover the nature of each, the idea of them held by the least educated of men is sufficient. I assume three definitions, or rather, three facts: one, *republican government is that in which the people as a body, or only a part of the people, have sovereign power; monarchical government is that in which one alone governs, but by fixed and established laws; whereas, in despotic government, one alone, without law and without rule, draws everything along by his will and his caprices.*[30]

Notice his inclusion of both democracy and aristocracy under the label of republic, and his definition of a monarchy as one which abides by laws, which is what distinguishes it from the rule of a despot. Also, Montesquieu distinguishes between the "nature" of a type of government and its "principle." "There is this difference between the nature of the government and its principle: its nature is that which makes it what it is, and its principle, that which makes it act. The one is its particular structure, and the other is the human passions that set it in motion."[31]

The particular principle that both democratic republics and aristocratic republics need is "virtue," although Montesquieu argues aristocracies need it less than democracies. "Just as there must be virtue in popular government, there must also be virtue in the aristocratic one. It is true that it is not as absolutely required."[32]

Montesquieu goes into considerable detail to specify just what kind of virtue he argues is necessary for a democratic republic to exist.

> One can define this virtue as love of the laws and the homeland. This love, requiring a continuous preference of the public interest over one's own, produces all the individual virtues; they are only that preference.
>
> This love is singularly connected with democracies. In them alone, government is entrusted to each citizen. Now government is like all things in the world; in order to preserve it, one must love it.[33]

Montesquieu also provides, and argues in favor of, a specific definition of "liberty" as part of his presentation of what a government is like when people have a country in which they can enjoy liberty. First of all, liberty does "not" mean just doing whatever one chooses to do:

It is true that in democracies the people seem to do what they want, but political liberty in no way consists in doing what one wants. In a state, that is, in a society where there are laws, liberty can consist only having the power to do what one should want to do and in no way being constrained to do what one should not want to do.

One must put oneself in mind of what independence is and what liberty is. Liberty is the right to do everything the laws permit; and if one citizen could do what they forbid, he would no longer have liberty because the others would likewise have this same power.[34]

Montesquieu does not automatically assign political liberty to republics or democracies. In fact, he states that quite often republics and democracies are less free than monarchies. This is due to his insistence that the exercise of power by any one person or group be constrained, or checked, by the power of other people or other groups.

Democracy and aristocracy are not free states by their nature. Political liberty is found only in moderate governments. But it is not always in moderate states. It is present only when power is not abused, but it has eternally been observed that any man who has power is led to abuse it; he continues until he finds limits.[35]

Most countries, according to Montesquieu, did not have political liberty as their purpose, not even the Italian republics of his day. The only country he considered as having political liberty as its purpose was Great Britain, because there, political power was divided between different branches of government. The influence of this distinction on the U.S. Constitution and its division of power between executive, legislative and judicial powers is of course well known.

Political liberty in a citizen is that tranquility of spirit which comes from the opinion each one has of his security, and in order for him to have this liberty the government must be such that one citizen cannot fear another citizen.

When legislative power is united with executive power in a single person or in a single body of the magistracy, there is no liberty, because one can fear that the same monarch or senate that makes tyrannical laws will execute them tyrannically.

Nor is there liberty if the power of judging is not separate from legislative power and from executive power.[36]

David Hume, even though his role was more that of a foil than of a source of inspiration because of his support for the monarchy and his preference for tradition rather than innovation, nevertheless was a widely read, and even cited, author during the early decades of the United States, as again Donald Lutz has shown.[37] Even though Hume was hesitant to recommend any changes to political institutions, he nevertheless did ponder the possibility of exploring the idea of an ideal form of government against which current forms could be compared so as to provide a kind of model for alterations.

> First, a legislature is essential, but not a unicameral legislature:
> All free governments must consist of two councils, lesser and greater; or, in other words, of a senate and people. The people, as HARRINGTON observes, would want wisdom, without the senate: The senate, without the people, would want honesty.[38]

Interestingly, Hume precedes later individuals such as Madison in arguing that it is possible to extend a republic over a large country. In fact, Hume argues that if done properly, a large republic would have distinct advantages over a small one.

> We shall conclude this subject, with observing the falsehood of the common opinion, that no large state, such as FRANCE or GREAT BRITAIN, could ever be modelled into a commonwealth, but that such a form of government can only take place in a city or small territory. The contrary seems probable. Though it is more difficult to form a republican government in an extensive country than in a city; there is more facility, when once it is formed, of preserving it steady and uniform, without tumult and faction.[39]

In fact, Hume argues that such large countries are precisely the sort in which one can, slowly and cautiously to be sure, approach more refined and perhaps even ideal forms of government. "In a large government, which is modelled with masterly skill, there is compass and room enough to refine the democracy, from the lower people, who may be admitted into the first elections or first concoction of the commonwealth, to the higher magistrates, who direct all the movements."[40]

I conclude this discussion with an examination of John Trenchard and Thomas Gordon's *Cato's Letters*, which antedated the American Revolution by only a few decades. That *Cato's Letters* was widely read, appreciated, and used by the leaders of the American Revolution is already well known. They also, like others before mentioned, locate ultimate power in the people at large. "The first Principles of Power are in the People; and all the Projects of Men in Power ought to refer to the People, to aim solely at their Good, and end in it: And whoever will pretend to govern them without regarding them, will soon repent it."[41]

The only form of government that can be called good according to Trenchard and Gordon is the one which aims at the common good, rather than the good of one or of a few.

> Dominion that is not maintained by the Sword, must be maintained by Consent; and in this latter Case, what Security can any Man at the Head of Affairs expect, but from pursuing the People's Welfare, and seeking their good Will? The Government of One for the Sake of One, is Tyranny; and so is the Government of a Few for the Sake of Themselves: But the Government executed for the Good of All, and with the Consent of All, is Liberty; and the Word (Government) is prophaned, and its Meaning abused, when it signifies any Thing else.[42]

The only form of government which does actively seek the good of all is the government that dutifully represents all of the people. That form of government is the mixed constitution, because it in turn represents the people at large, the aristocracy, and the monarchy, all at the same time rather than any one at a time.

> But, Thanks be to Heaven and our worthy Ancestors, our Liberties are better secured. We have a Constitution, in which the People have a large Share: They are one part of the Legislature, and have the sole Power of giving Money; which includes in it every thing that they can ask for the publick Good; and the Representatives, being neither awed nor bribed, will always act for the Country's Interest; their own being so interwoven with the People's Happiness, that they must stand and fall together.[43]

Any form of good government must also be one in which the laws are the ultimate power. Rule of law, rather than rule by any one person or group, is for Trenchard and Gordon an essential aspect of the good government the people of Great Britain enjoy.

> Power is like Fire; it warms, scorches, or destroys, according as it is watched, provoked, or increased. It is as dangerous as useful. Its only Rule is the Good of the People; but because it is apt to break its Bounds, in all good Governments nothing, or as little as may be, ought to be left to Chance, or the Humors of Men in Authority: All should proceed by fixed and stated Rules; and upon any Emergency, new Rules should be made. This is the Constitution, and this the Happiness of *Englishmen*, as has been formerly shewn at large in these Letters.[44]

All of the above approach the topic of a republic from the classical notion of what a republic should, or needs, to be like. Ideas like a focus on agriculture as the primary way for citizens to earn a living contrast sharply with the realities of American life from even the colonial era. I argue it was simply no longer possible for the American Revolution to have resulted in a classical republic, given the already established ways of making a living the colonists had adopted. This is in keeping with recent scholarship on the origins of the American Revolution.

It is precisely this departure from classical conceptions of a republic toward more commercial ones that T.H. Breen argues allowed the American Revolution to occur in the first place. In stark contrast to approaches which have emphasized the ideological influences of the American Revolution, Breen argues it was the shared experience of buying and selling in the Atlantic marketplace which created a common American sense of identity.

> What gave the American Revolution distinctive shape was an earlier transformation of the Anglo-American consumer marketplace. This event, which some historians have called a "consumer revolution," commenced sometime during the middle of the eighteenth century, and as modestly wealthy families acquired ever larger quantities of British manufactures—for the most part everyday goods that made life warmer, more comfortable, more sanitary, or perhaps simply more enjoyable—the face of material culture changed dramatically. Suddenly, buyers voiced concerns about color and texture, about fashion and etiquette, and about making the right choices from among an expanding number of possibilities.
>
> This was surely not a society of self-sufficient yeoman farmers. People purchased the items they most desired at local stores; they often demanded and received liberal credit. Each year the volume of imports increased, creating by 1750 a virtual "empire of goods." England experienced the same consumer revolution as did the American colonists. But there was a major difference. In a colonial marketplace in which dependency was always an issue, imported goods had the potential to become politicized, turning familiar imported items such as cloth and tea into symbols of imperial oppression. And since Americans from Savannah to Portsmouth purchased the same general range of goods, they found that they were able to communicate with each other about a common experience. Whatever their differences, they were consumers in an empire that seemed determined to compromise their rights and liberties.
>
> *The Marketplace of Revolution* argues, therefore, that the colonists' shared experience as consumers provided them with the cultural resources needed to develop a bold new form of political protest.[45]

Joyce Appleby argues that commercial success was essential to the survival of the early Republic and also that both Federalist and Democratic-Republicans, whether they realized it or not, were advocates of a commercial conception of a republic, rather than one based on classical ideas.

> In contrast to these characterizations of early national attitudes, I shall argue that the new European demand for American grains—the crops produced by most farm families from Virginia through Maryland, Pennsylvania, Delaware, New Jersey, New York, and up the Connecticut River Valley—created an unusually favorable opportunity for ordinary men to produce for the Atlantic trade world. Far from being viewed apprehensively, this prospect during the thirty years following the adoption of the Constitution undergirded Jefferson's

> optimism about America's future as a progressive, prosperous, democratic nation. Indeed, this anticipated participation in an expanding international commerce in foodstuffs created the material base for a new social vision owing little conceptually or practically to antiquity, the Renaissance, or the mercantilists of eighteenth century England. From this perspective, the battle between the Jeffersonians and Federalists appears not as a conflict between the patrons of agrarian self-sufficiency and the proponents of modern commerce, but rather as a struggle between two different elaborations of capitalistic development in America. Jefferson becomes, not the heroic loser in a battle against modernity, but the conspicuous winner in a contest over how the government should serve its citizens in the first generation of the nation's territorial expansion.[46]

Gordon S. Wood makes a similar argument in pointing to the departure from the traditional distinction between gentlemen and laborers that occurred during the early decades of the United States. Those responsible for the transformation of the American economy were not those traditional gentlemen, such as Hamilton, who did not work with their hands, but rather those we now identify as businesspeople.

> We make a big mistake thinking that capitalism was created mainly by Alexander Hamilton and a few stock-jobbers, speculators, and wealthy merchants. If any group was most responsible for the burgeoning capitalist economy of the early republic, it was the Republicans and all the commercially minded artisans and farmers who were striving to get ahead—"laboring" men like Walter Brewster, Christopher Leffingwell, and William Manning.[47]

Paul A. Gilje emphasizes the mental changes that helped lead to the creation of the more commercial, rather than classical, republic of the United States. In other words, how did Americans in general come to think in capitalistic ways, rather than those based on traditional, hierarchical society, is the point of his argument.

> Ultimately, the impact of the American Revolution on capitalism had its greatest effect on the individual. The American Revolution transformed the social landscape from a world that emphasized hierarchy and communal goals, to a world marked by equality and individualism—from classical to liberal republicanism.[48]

NOTES

1. J.G.A. Pocock, *The Machiavellian Moment: Florentine Political Thought and the Atlantic Republican Tradition* (Princeton: Princeton University Press, 1975), 77.

2. Polybius, *The Histories*, trans. by Robin Waterfield (Oxford: Oxford University Press, 2010), 373.
3. Ibid, 384.
4. Cicero, *On the Commonwealth*, trans. by George Holland Sabine and Stanley Barney Smith (New York: MacMillan Publishing Company, 1976), 131.
5. Ibid, 134.
6. Niccolo Machiavelli, *The Prince and the Discourses*, trans. by Luigi Ricci, revised by E.R.P. Vincent (New York: The Modern Library, 1950), 114–115.
7. Ibid, 115–116.
8. J.G.A. Pocock, *The Machiavellian Moment: Florentine Political Thought and the Atlantic Republican Tradition* (Princeton: Princeton University Press, 1975), 184.
9. Ibid, 361.
10. Thomas Hobbes, *Leviathan*, ed. by Richard Tuck (Cambridge: Cambridge University Press, 1991), 131.
11. Ibid, 131.
12. James Harrington, *The Commonwealth of Oceana and A System of Politics*, ed. by J.G.A. Pocock (Cambridge: Cambridge University Press, 1992), 4–5.
13. Ibid, 12.
14. Ibid, 22.
15. Ibid, 34.
16. John Locke, *The Two Treatises of Government*, ed. by Peter Laslett (Cambridge: Cambridge University Press, 1988), 355–356.
17. Ibid, 367.
18. Ibid, 412.
19. Algernon Sidney, *Discourses Concerning Government*, ed. by Thomas G. West (Indianapolis: Liberty Classics, 1990), 30–31.
20. Ibid, 99.
21. Ibid, 166.
22. Ibid, 175.
23. Ibid, 189.
24. Ibid, 191.
25. Ibid, 192.
26. Ibid, 196.
27. Ibid, 519.
28. Ibid, 519.
29. Donald Lutz, "The Relative Influence of European Writers on Late Eighteenth Century American Political Thought," *The American Political Science Review* 78, no. 1 (1984): 189–197.
30. Charles-Louis de Secondat, Baron de la Brede et de Montesquieu, *The Spirit of the Laws*, trans. and ed. by Anne M. Cohler, Basia Carolyn Miller, and Harold Samuel Stone (Cambridge: Cambridge University Press, 1989), 10.
31. Ibid, 21.
32. Ibid, 24.
33. Ibid, 36.
34. Ibid, 155.

35. Ibid, 155–156.
36. Ibid, 156–157.
37. Donald Lutz, "The Relative Influence of European Writers on Late Eighteenth Century American Political Thought." *The American Political Science Review* 78, no. 1 (1984): 189–197.
38. David Hume, "Idea of a Perfect Commonwealth," in *Essays, Moral, Political, and Literary*, ed. by Eugene F. Miller (Indianapolis: Liberty Fund, 1987), 522–523.
39. Ibid, 527.
40. Ibid, 528.
41. John Trenchard and Thomas Gordon, *Cato's Letters*, third edition (New York: Russell & Russell, 1969), 179.
42. Ibid, 179–180.
43. Ibid, 181.
44. Ibid, 192.
45. T.H. Breen, *The Marketplace of Revolution: How Consumer Politics Shaped American Independence* (New York: Oxford University Press, 2004), xv.
46. Joyce Appleby, "Commercial Farming and the 'Agrarian Myth' in the Early Republic," *The Journal of American History* 68, no. 4 (March 1982): 836.
47. Gordon S. Wood, "The Enemy Is Us: Democratic Capitalism in the Early Republic," *Journal of the Early Republic* 16, no. 2 (Summer 1996): 304.
48. Paul A. Gilje, "The Rise of Capitalism in the Early Republic," *Journal of the Early Republic* 16, no. 2 (Summer, 1996): 178.

Chapter Two

Hamilton and Madison on Slavery

Slavery, the glaring example of hypocrisy in the American Revolution, is an issue which has affected American life in countless ways to this day. Numerous scholars have commented on the issue of slavery and the Founders, so before I turn to my presentation of Hamilton and Madison, I first present a brief account of the work completed by others thus far.

Mark D. McGarvie has written on Jefferson and slavery. Now, of course, this book is not about Jefferson, but his argument does, I think, add value to attempts to understand why so many were able to on the one hand advocate for freedom and liberty, but on the other hand do little to nothing to advocate for an end to slavery.

> Jefferson's belief in the importance of form, evident in his architectural and musical preferences, and even in his personal relationships, is less obvious in his commitment to law as the means of social governance. In this commitment he epitomizes the Enlightenment modernist's acceptance of form as liberalizing. In the same way that the symmetry of Mozart's compositions or the American adaptation of classical columns or friezes reflected the limits upon man's reason posed by taste and judgment, the founding father's dependence upon law reflected a recognition of liberty restrained by the need for social order. Only when the parameters of taste, judgment, order, or virtue were accepted could man truly be free to pursue the limits of his reason. In this way law restrained policy initiatives that could legitimately be pursued to achieve social goals.[1]

Thus, McGarvie argues, Jefferson was restrained by the other Enlightenment ideas he cherished as far as what he felt he could do about slavery. Ending slavery would have to come through change in public sentiment, and that, according to Jefferson, could only come about through improved education. It seems to me that Madison can also be seen in this light, especially given the close partnership he had with Jefferson. Hamilton, on the other hand, had no such connection to Jefferson, and this helps account for his very different approach to slavery.

Kenneth Morgan has written on George Washington and slavery and came to quite different conclusions than McGarvie as to why Washington did not free his slaves during his lifetime, although the slaves he personally owned were set free in his will.

> It is apparent that Washington expressed a fair amount of dissatisfaction with the system of chattel slavery. Why, it must be asked, did he not free his slaves during his lifetime? To answer this question, one needs to look at the private and public contexts of his life. The private reasons for Washington's disinclination to sell or free his slaves stemmed not so much from a commitment to running Mount Vernon profitably, for we have noted the surplus labourers there, but from his genuine difficulty about envisaging the conditions under which slaves could be freed. The two views were inextricably linked in his thinking; the agriculturist and the businessman was never disentangled from the slaveowner. Washington's commercial outlook made him conceive of slaves as chattel upon whose head a price could be calculated; and, despite his protestations about being overstocked with slaves, he did not intend to diminish or lose what to him was an important investment, unless he benefitted financially.[2]

Now, Morgan does go on to note that Washington was also concerned enough about national unity and the potential any public statement he might have made in favor of ending slavery to undermine said unity. It is genuinely the case that there were many such individuals who thought of slaves only as their property, something that could never legally be taken away from them and would tear the country apart rather than give them up.

Kenneth R. Bowling makes precisely this point. In discussing the Compromise of 1790, which led to the decision to locate the permanent U.S. capital on the Potomac, its location in a part of the country much friendlier to slavery than either New York City or Philadelphia, clearly played a role.

> Because of the silence of the founders, historians, myself included, were slow to recognize the role of slavery in the Compromise of 1790, the first of the three. From 1783, when the question of a location for the federal seat of government first became public, until 1790, when it was resolved, southerners tenaciously fought—even threatening disunion—for a location that would reflect and protect their culture and institutions, the most prominent of which was slavery. If the national seat were located in the South, they reasoned, newspapers, federal officeholders, and the government itself would tend to reflect the southern viewpoint. One does not have to live in Washington, DC to know that it remained a southern city until the second half of the 20th century.[3]

Slavery was spoken of by both over several decades of their lives, and each took a quite different approach in responding to the problem of slavery. Neither Hamilton nor Madison was actually in favor of slavery, but as I will show, Hamilton was far more active in opposing slavery, and even seeking its discontinuation, while Madison was much more equivocal in his response. Madison did not speak out publicly in favor of ending slavery until near the end of his life, while Hamilton took a far more active, public role as early as during the Revolutionary War.

From Hamilton we will see an effort during the Revolution, along with his friend and fellow Army officer Henry Laurens, to actively recruit slaves for the Army, and offer them their freedom in exchange for service. He simply did not think that slaves were either better or worse than other ordinary people. That he maintained this point of view throughout the remainder of his life we will clearly see by his extremely active involvement in the New York Manumission Society up until the time of his duel with Aaron Burr.

Madison, on the other hand, even though as we will see, found the idea of freeing slaves in exchange for military service a good idea, never adopted an active role in ridding the United States of slavery. Only late in life did he even half-heartedly "recommend" an effort to resettle slaves who had been voluntarily freed back in Africa. Indeed, he remained convinced throughout his life that blacks and whites could not peacefully and successfully coexist in the United States

Now, we do know Hamilton clearly opposed slavery from at least the time of the Revolutionary War, because he stated such in his correspondence. Clearly, Hamilton did not believe Africans were inferior to Europeans. He unequivocally said so as part of the plan he and his friend, Lt. Colonel Henry Laurens developed to organize battalions of slave soldiers, who would as a result of their service gain their freedom.

> Colonel Laurens, who will have the honor of delivering you this letter, is on his way to South Carolina, on a project, which I think, in the present situation of affairs there, is a very good one and deserves every kind of support and encouragement. This is to raise two three or four batalions of negroes; with the assistance of the government of that state, by contributions from the owners in proportion to the number they possess. . . .
>
> It appears to me, that an expedient of this kind, in the present state of Southern affairs, is the most rational, that can be adopted, and promises very important advantages. . . . I mention this, because I frequently hear it objected to the scheme of embodying negroes that they are too stupid to make soldiers. This is so far from appearing to me a valid objection that I think their want of cultivation (for their natural faculties are probably as good as ours) joined to that habit of subordination which they acquire from a life of servitude, will make them sooner become soldiers than our White inhabitants. Let officers be men of sense and sentiment, and the nearer the soldiers approach to machines perhaps the better.[4]

I realize this is a lengthy quote, but since I am basing my arguments entirely on what both Hamilton and Madison actually wrote, in this instance its length is necessary. Here, we see clearly Hamilton's enthusiasm for a way of at least reducing the number of slaves in the United States, in part to make use of their services instead of the British, his clear opinion that Africans are not inferior to Europeans, and finally his emotional preference for the removal of slavery.

Madison also thought it a good idea to offer freedom to slaves in exchange for military service during the Revolution.

> I am glad to find the legislature persist in their resolution to recruit their line of the army for the war, though without deciding on the expediency of the mode under their consideration, would it not be as well to liberate and make soldiers at once of the blacks themselves as to make them instruments for enlisting white Soldiers?[5]

As I mentioned above, Madison did express a desire to distance himself from slavery, at least in his personal life. "My wish is if possible to provide a decent & independent subsistence, without encountering the difficulties which I foresee in that line. Another of my wishes is to depend as little as possible on the labour of slaves. The difficulty of reconciling these views, has brought into my thoughts several projects from which advantage seemed attainable."[6]

Nevertheless, he continued to make use of slaves, even when away from home, where he had numerous slaves working in various capacities on his plantation. Concerning a slave that had run away, and a slave currently in his service, he stated in a letter to his father:

> The enquiries which I have at different times made of Billey concerning Anthony satisfy me that he either knows, or will tell nothing of the matter. It does not appear to me probable that all the circumstances mentioned by Anthony with regard to his rambles can be true.[7]

One of his reasons for not actively seeking the end of slavery was the Union of all the states was more important than ending slavery. Since some states were implacable on the subject of emancipation, he placed the maintenance and continuation of the United States as a whole above any effort at ending slavery.

> I should conceive this clause to be impolitic, if it were one of those things which could be excluded without encountering greater evils. The southern states would not have entered into the union of America, without the temporary permission

> of that trade. And if they were excluded from the union, the consequences might be dreadful to them and to us.[8]

Also:

> Great as the evil is, a dismemberment of the union would be worse. If those states should disunite from the other states, for not indulging them in the temporary continuance of this traffic, they might solicit and obtain aid from foreign powers.[9]

Madison was, however, never actively in favor of extending the slave trade any longer than necessary. Article 1, Section 9 of the Constitution specifically prohibited Congress from outlawing the importation of slaves until 1808, but it did allow Congress to impose a tax on such importation in the meantime. In a speech on the floor of the House of Representatives, he said:

> I conceive the constitution in this particular, was formed in order that the government, whilst it was restrained from laying a total prohibition, might be able to give some testimony of the sense of America, with respect to the African trade. We have liberty to impose a tax or duty upon the importation of such persons as any of the states now existing shall think proper to admit.[10]

And:

> I do not wish to say anything harsh, to the hearing of gentlemen who entertain different sentiments from me, or different sentiments from those I represent, but if there is any one point in which it is clearly the policy of this nation, so far as we constitutionally can, to vary the practice obtaining under some of the state governments it is this; therefore, upon principle, we ought to discountenance it as far as is in our power.[11]

Further, Madison added one of his reasons for opposing the continuance of the slave trade—that it would weaken the national security of not just the slave states, but of the United States as a whole. Thus, rather than being a states' rights issue regarding their internal police, further importation of slaves was a threat to the entire United States, and given the federal government's requirement in the Constitution to protect each and every state from invasion, this issue became one proper for the federal government to take action on. It would have been interesting to see the effect of this if he had been a more public advocate of the effect of slavery on national security overriding states' rights.

> If I was not afraid of being told that the representatives of the several states, are the best able to judge of what is proper and conducive to their particular

> prosperity, I should venture to say that it is as much the interest of Georgia and South Carolina, as of any in the union. Every addition they receive to their number of slaves, tends to weaken them and renders them less capable of self defence; in case of hostilities with foreign nations, they will be the means of inviting attack instead of repelling invasion.[12]

This is a point both Hamilton and Madison had made during the Revolutionary War, and both remembered those lessons learned in their later political careers. As students of the later American Civil War have demonstrated, the large slave population was at first a drag on the Confederacy's war efforts, because so many potential troops had to be kept at home rather than on the front lines in order to keep slaves under control, but later freed slaves provided essential services, both under arms and in other ways, to the Union Army. Clearly, this issue is one on which both Hamilton and Madison were prescient, but not in the way either expected.

Madison did entertain the idea of a more voluntary form of emancipation through the settlement of freed slaves in Africa, primarily because he did not think people of European descent would ever genuinely accept those of African descent. He simply did not believe they could coexist, in stark contrast to Hamilton. The only option he ever supported, at least in theory, was colonization.

> Without enquiring into the practicability or the most proper means of establishing a Settlement of freed blacks on the Coast of Africa, it may be remarked as one motive to the benevolent experiment that if such an asylum was provided, it might prove a great encouragement to manumission in the Southern parts of the U.S. and even afford the best hope yet presented of putting an end to the slavery in which not less than 600,000 unhappy negroes are now involved.[13]

And:

> In order to render this change eligible as well to the Society as to the Slaves, it would be necessary that a compleat incorporation of the latter into the former should result from the act of manumission. This is rendered impossible by the prejudices of the Whites, prejudices which proceeding principally from the difference of colour must be considered as permanent and insuperable.
>
> It only remains then that some proper external receptacle be provided for the slaves who obtain their liberty. . . . The result then is that an experiment for providing such an external establishment for the blacks as might induce the humanity of Masters, and by degrees both the humanity & policy of the Governments, to forward the abolition of slavery in America, ought to be pursued on the Coast of Africa or in some other foreign situation.[14]

As I have mentioned above, Madison was equivocal on the issue of slavery throughout his life. He clearly did not approve of slavery itself, but was not convinced, as Hamilton was, that it was possible to both end slavery and have former slaves live peacefully alongside former slave owners and others of European descent. In contrast to active slave advocates, however, he emphatically did not believe slavery to be in any way a good influence on society.

> The Petitions on the subject of Slavery have employed more than a week, and are still before the Committee of the whole. The Gentlemen from S. Carolina & Georgia are intemperate beyond all example and even all decorum. They are not content with palliating slavery as a deep-rooted abuse, but plead for the lawfulness of the African trade itself—nor with protesting agst. the object of the Memorials, but lavish the most virulent language on the authors of them.[15]

However, Madison also did not think it proper, or possible, for him as an elected official to speak out against the institution of slavery as such, given the number of his constituents who, like he, owned slaves. In a letter to Robert Pleasants during his time serving in Congress under the Articles of Confederation, he stated:

> Animadversions, such as it contains and which the authorized object of the petitioners did not require on the slavery existing in our country, are supposed by the holders of that species of property, to lessen the value by weakening the tenure of it. Those from whom I derive my public station are known by me to be greatly interested in that species of property, and to view the matter in that light. It would seem that I might be chargeable at least with want of candour, if not of fidelity, were I to make use of a situation in which their confidence has placed me, to become a volunteer in giving a public wound, as they would deem it, to an interest on which they set so great a value.[16]

So, what we see from this comparison of Hamilton and Madison on the issue of slavery is agreement on the evil of slavery, but wide divergence on just what to do about it, given their vastly different expectations for whether or not those of European descent could ever live peaceably with those of African descent. Hamilton was again far more active in opposing slavery, had essentially an equal view of the abilities of blacks versus whites, and continued his efforts from early on until the end of his life.

Madison, on the other hand, while personally deploring slavery, never actually took action, either privately or publicly, to oppose the institution itself. He remained a slave owner throughout his life, thought it improper to even indirectly associate himself with anti-slavery efforts while in political office, and only late in life made even the limited public statements regarding slavery. He just did not think whites would ever accept blacks, especially former slaves.

This disagreement between Hamilton and Madison is of course reflective of the much wider conflict over slavery in the United States, which was not resolved until the Civil War ended, and the issue of race relations is one which the United States, like almost every other country, still struggles with to this day.

As far as their conflicting visions of republicanism, these excerpts from the writings of Hamilton and Madison show that, for Hamilton, "liberty" meant liberty for *everyone*, including slaves. The American Revolution was an event Hamilton saw as demanding freedom for all Americans, not just those considered "white." Hamilton clearly did not consider there to be any underlying racial differences of importance between blacks and whites, which we saw in his opinion regarding the suitability of freed slaves for military service. Neither better nor worse than whites, freed slaves would have been an *asset*, not a threat to the republic. If nothing else, Hamilton was prescient in arguing that if the Americans did not make slaves the offer, the British would. For Hamilton, republicanism did not carry with it any racial component. Blacks and whites were in his estimation equal and could participate equally in the American republic as he envisioned it.

Any participation by both free blacks and whites in the American republic was, on the other hand, impossible for Madison. He disliked slavery but made use of slaves throughout his life. He did not, in contrast to some other Founders, ever free his slaves. Finally, even his belated effort of supporting resettling voluntarily freed slaves reflected only his unwavering belief that blacks and whites simply could not successfully live together as equals. For Madison, the American republic did have a racial component, whites only, as part of his vision for its success.

NOTES

1. Mark D. McGarvie, "'In perfect accordance with his character': Thomas Jefferson, Slavery, and the Law," *Indiana Magazine of History* 95, no. 2 (June 1999): 142.

2. Kenneth Morgan, "George Washington and the Problem of Slavery," *Journal of American Studies* 34, no. 2 (August 2000): 288.

3. Kenneth R. Bowling, "The Silence of the Founders," *Washington History* 32, no. ½ (Fall 2020): 58.

4. Harold C. Syrett, ed., and Jacob Ed. Cooke, assoc. ed., *The Papers of Alexander Hamilton*, volume II: 1779–1781 (New York: Columbia University Press, 1961), 17–19.

5. William T. Hutchinson, and William M.E. Rachal, eds., *The Papers of James Madison*, Volume 2: 20 March 1780–23 February 1781 (Chicago: The University of Chicago Press, 1962), 209–211.
6. Robert A. Rutland, et. al, eds., *The Papers of James Madison*, Volume 8: 10 March 1784–28 March 1786 (Chicago, The University of Chicago Press, 1973), 328.
7. Robert A. Rutland, et.al, eds., *The Papers of James Madison*, Volume 10: 27 May 1787–3 March 1788 (Chicago: The University of Chicago Press, 1977), 118.
8. Robert A. Rutland, et.al, eds., *The Papers of James Madison*, Volume 11: 7 March 1788–1 March 1789 (Chicago: The University of Chicago Press, 1977), 150.
9. Ibid, 151.
10. Charles F. Hobson, et.al, eds., *The Papers of James Madison*, Volume 12: 2 March 1789–20 January 1790, with a supplement 24 October 1775–24 January 1789 (Chicago: The University of Chicago Press, 1979), 161.
11. Ibid, 162.
12. Ibid.
13. Charles F. Hobson, et.al, eds., *The Papers of James Madison*, Volume 12: 2 March 1789–20 January 1790, with a supplement 24 October 1775–24 January 1789 (Chicago: The University of Chicago Press, 1979), 437–438.
14. Ibid.
15. Charles F. Hobson, et.al, eds., *The Papers of James Madison*, Volume 13: 20 January 1790–31 March 1791 (Chicago: The University of Chicago Press, 1981), 109.
16. Robert A. Rutland, et.al, eds., *The Papers of James Madison*, Volume 14: 6 April 1791–16 March 1793 (Chicago: The University of Chicago Press, 1983), 91–92.

Chapter Three

Hamilton and Madison on France versus Great Britain

Stanley Elkins and Eric McKitrick in their *The Age of Federalism*, argue that the later political differences between Hamilton and Madison can be explained largely by Hamilton's Anglophilia and Madison's Anglophobia. I respectfully disagree and will argue that Hamilton and Madison's differences in regard to overall foreign policy, when each had the opportunity to weigh in on that issue, were not attributable to a strong preference by either for the two great powers of that time.

We will see Hamilton's focus was on American independence from both Great Britain and France, and not on maintaining ties with Great Britain at any cost out of some "Anglophilia." In each case, when the potential of war loomed, first with Great Britain, later with France, he counseled the exact same approach: Prepare for war at home, but first try to negotiate a solution before resorting to a declaration of war. Hamilton also at first supported the French Revolution, but had doubts all along, which were for him confirmed by the Terror and other assorted violence, and especially by the execution of Louis XVI. That did turn him away from actively supporting France, but not toward greater support for Great Britain in response.

With Madison, we will see him of two different minds regarding Great Britain and France at various points. At first, after the Revolution, he did clearly favor France, out of both a sense of gratitude for French assistance and also out of a strong antipathy toward Great Britain. Then, when the French Revolution occurred, he did show a continued preference for France out of a spirit of worldwide republican revolution. It is only with Napoleon's takeover that he abandoned France, not in preference for Great Britain, but rather toward a much cooler attitude toward both countries.

I argue Hamilton had, rather than Anglophilia, a staunch commitment to the United States. His commitment sometimes seems to me to be such that only converts to a cause or religion manifest, but that can be traced to his birth in the Caribbean rather than in any state. Thus, in comparison with Madison, his credentials as an American were based far more on his deeds, rather than simply being part of his identity. In a letter to George Washington during 1783, he stated:

> We have I fear men [among] us and men in trust who have a hankering afte[r] British connection. We have others whose confidence in France savours of credulity. The intrigues of the former and the incautiousness of the latter may be both, though in different degrees, injurious to the American interests; and make it difficult for prudent men to steer a proper course.[1]

So, even before the later conflicts of the 1790s, Hamilton was himself concerned about the possible influence of Great Britain and France. Here, he clearly states his goal is to "steer a proper course," not as an adherent to either great power, but rather to find an American way of proceeding.

Further, he was also concerned with European influence in general over the United States, and of course wanted to avoid such an occurrence. In another letter to George Washington from 1783, he remarked:

> Your Excellency will before this reaches you have received a letter from the Marquis De la Fayette informing you that the preliminaries of peace between all the belligerent powers have been concluded. I congratulate your Excellency on this happy conclusion of your labours. It now only remains to make solid establishments within to perpetuate our union to prevent our being a ball in the hands of European powers bandied against each other at their pleasure—in fine to make our independence truly a blessing. This it is to be lamented will be an arduous work, for to borrow a figure from mechanics, the centrifugal is much stronger than the centripetal force in these states—the seeds of disunion much more numerous than those of union.[2]

Regarding the French Revolution, Hamilton made it clear in a letter to the Marquis de Lafayette during 1789 that he was, at first, quite happy with that event, but that he did have fears all along about possible outcomes of the Revolution. He hoped the French would not make too many changes, given his assessment of what he considered the French "character," and also what he considered possible, due to his understanding of human nature. Notably, Hamilton also expressed concern regarding the influence of French philosophers.

> I have seen with a mixture of Pleasure and apprehension the Progress of the events which have lately taken Place in your Country. As a friend to mankind and to liberty I rejoice in the efforts which you are making to establish it while I fear much for the final success of the attempts, for the fate of those I esteem who

> are engaged in it, and for the danger in case of success of innovations greater than will consist with the real felicity of your Nation.[3]

In fact, Hamilton sought parity in trade for the United States with both Great Britain and France. In a letter to Thomas Jefferson during 1791, he wrote:

> I had rather endeavour by a new Treaty of Commerce with France to extend reciprocal advantages and fix them on a permanent basis. . . . My commercial system turns very much on giving a free course to Trade and cultivating good humour with all the world. And I feel a particular reluctance to hazard any thing in the present state of our affairs which may lead to commercial warfare with any power; which as far as my knowledge of examples extends is commonly productive of mutual inconvenience and injury and of dispositions tending to a worse kind of warfare.[4]

For Hamilton, the point, and value, of good relations with Great Britain would be the bargaining strength it would give the United States with the rest of Europe. In a letter to Benjamin Goodhue during 1791 he mentioned,

> I would not warrant the issue; but if some liberal arrangement with Great Britain should ensue, it will have a prodigious effect upon the Conduct of some other parts of Europe. Tis however most wise for us to depend as little as possible upon European Caprice & to exert ourselves to the utmost to unfold and improve every domestic resource.[5]

In regard to establishing and maintaining a foreign policy based on neutrality between warring European powers, Hamilton argued this approach would be the best way to retire the Revolutionary War debt as fast as possible. In a letter to George Washington from 1792 he wrote:

> The public Debt was produced by the late war. It is not the fault of the present government that it exists; unless it can be proved, that public morality and policy do not require of a Government an honest provision for its debts. . . . If the policy of the Country be prudent, cautious and *neutral* towards foreign nations, there is a rational probability, that war may be avoided long enough to wipe off the debt. . . . But whether the public Debt shall be extinguished or not within a moderate period depends on the temper of the people.[6]

So, far from being based on a preference for relations with Great Britain, Hamilton's policies were aimed at greater strength and stability for the United States, in part by paying off its indebtedness as soon as could be by staying out of wars as long as possible.

Further evidence of Hamilton's strictly American views can be seen in an article he wrote for the *Gazette of the United States* in 1793.

> The late War with Great Britain produced three parties in the UStates, an *English* party, a *French* Party, and an *American* party, if the latter can with propriety be called a party. These parties continue to the present moment. There are persons among us, who appear to be more alive to the interests of France, on the one hand, and to those of Great Britain, on the other, than to those of the UStates. Both these dispositions are to be condemned, and will be rejected by every true American.
>
> A dispassionate and virtuous citizen of the UStates will scorn to stand on any but purely *American* ground. It will be his study to render his feeling and affections neutral and impartial towards all foreign Nations. His prayer will be for peace, and that his country may be as much as possible kept out of the destructive vortex of foreign politics.[7]

In his *Defense of the President's Neutrality Proclamation* from May 1793, Hamilton first stated what had caused his support for the French Revolution to weaken and then disappear. Also, he indicated for the first time his concern that such "French" influence might even negatively affect the United States as well.

> That zeal for the liberty of mankind, which produced so universal a sympathy in the cause of France in the first stages of its revolution, and which, it is supposed, has not yet yielded to the just reprobation, which a sober temperate and humane people, friends of religion, social order, and justice, enemies to tumult and massacre, to the wanton and lawless shedding of human blood cannot but bestow upon those extravagancies excesses and outrages, which have sullied and which endanger that cause—that laudable, it is not too much to say that holy zeal is intended by every art of misrepresentation and deception to be made the instrument first of controuling finally of overturning the Government of the Union.[8]

When as a result of British attacks on American shipping after the outbreak of war with revolutionary France, many called for the United States to join the war on France's side, Hamilton urged President Washington to negotiate first, but also to have the United States prepare for war. Hamilton clearly shows a willingness to go to war if needed, but not a desire to avoid war with Great Britain at all cost out of some preference for that country. In a letter to George Washington during 1794, he argued:

> A course of accurate observation has impressed on my mind a full conviction, that there exist in our councils three considerable parties—one decided for preserving peace by every effort which shall any way consist with the ultimate maintenance of the national honor and rights and disposed to cultivate with all nations a friendly understanding. . . .
>
> The views of the first party in respect to the questions between GBritain and us favour the following course of conduct—To take effectual measures

of military preparation, creating in earnest force and revenue—to vest the President with important powers respecting navigation and commerce for ulterior contingencies—to endeavour by another effort of negotiation confided to hands able to manage it and friendly to the object, to obtain reparation for the wrongs we suffer and a demarkation of a line of conduct to govern in future. . . . If that experiment fails then and not till then to resort to reprisals and war. . . .

> At no moment were the indications of a plan on the part of Great Britain to go to War with us sufficiently decisive to preclude the hope of averting it by a negotiation conducted with prudent energy and seconded by such military preparations as should be demonstrative of a Resolution eventually to vindicate our rights.[9]

Note Hamilton's main points: The United States should avoid war if possible, but should be ready should there be no other option; Great Britain has not itself declared war, and has not shown a clear intention of doing so; and finally, war is an extremely uncertain state for any country to be in, let alone a young country such as the United States. His concerns do not include maintaining peace with Great Britain at any cost, but rather what he conceives the best options for the United States to be.

He did make his disillusionment with France clear, though, in his work *The Cause of France*, in which he compares the behavior of France's new rulers with that of religious fanatics.

> The world has been scourged with many fanatical sects in religion—who inflamed by a sincere but mistaken zeal have perpetuated under the idea of serving God the most atrocious crimes. . . .
>
> But even this comparison is too favourable to the ruling party in France. Judging from their acts, we are authorised to pronounce the cause in which they are engaged, not the cause of Liberty, but the cause of Vice Atheism and Anarchy.[10]

Hamilton was clearly one of those who were afraid of French influence, and of the United States becoming one of its satellites as had several countries in Europe. In a letter to William Bradford in 1795, he complained: "When shall we cease to consider ourselves as a colony to France?"[11] He quite clearly did not have such concerns about Great Britain, which may very well have contributed to his being characterized by his opponents as being in favor of too much influence for that country in contrast to France.

He was not, though, opposed to at least cordial relations with France if possible. In response to a request from George Washington for his thoughts on the recently negotiated Jay Treaty with Great Britain, Hamilton argued:

> But will it give umbrage to France?

> It cannot do it unless France is unreasonable.
>
> Because our engagements with her remain unimpaired & because she will still be upon as good a footing as Great Britain.[12]

Hamilton is clearly not of the mindset of preferring Great Britain over France, at least in commercial matters. If he had been, he would have sought greater trade privileges for Great Britain than France, and there is no record of his ever expressing such a desire or goal.

When later war with France appeared to be a possibility, Hamilton once again advocated policies which mirrored his earlier preferences for avoiding war with Great Britain: preparedness at home but making every possible effort to avoid war first. He even suggested that any group of extraordinary envoys to France include James Madison, whom he had by this point known for years to be a critic, in order to show no partiality toward Great Britain. To William Loughton Smith he wrote in 1797:

> I am clearly of opinion for an extraordinary mission and as clearly it should embrace *Madison*. . . . I would accumulate the proofs of French Violence & demonstrate to all our Citizens that nothing possible has been omitted. . . . The idea is a plausible one that as we sent an Envoy Extraordinary to Britain so ought we to send one to France.[13]

Again in 1797, Hamilton expressed a desire for, instead of preference for either Great Britain or France, a genuinely American way of understanding the United States' standing as regards the various European powers. To George Washington he wrote:

> We have nothing new here more than our papers contain; but are anxiously looking forward to a further development of the negotiations in Europe with an ardent desire for general accomodation. It is at the same time agreeable to observe that the public mind is adopting more and more sentiments truly American and free from foreign tincture.[14]

Hamilton, like Madison, corresponded with the Marquis de Lafayette. It is noteworthy that the Marquis did try to counsel each side in the American debate at that time to give each other the benefit of the doubt, but neither was willing to listen, unfortunately. In any case, Hamilton did express his views to the Marquis regarding France, its revolution, Great Britain, whether or not France was capable of being a republic like the United States, and the charges against him of Anglophilia. In 1798 he wrote:

> The suspension of the King and the massacre of September (of which events a temporary intelligence was received in this Country) cured me of my good will for the French Revolution.
>
> I have never been able to believe that France can make a republic and I have believed that the attempt while it continues can only produce misfortunes. . . .
>
> I shall only assure you that a disposition to form an intimate connection with Great Britain, which is charged upon us forms no part of the real Cause, though it has served the purpose of a party to impose its belief of it on france. . . . The basis of the policy of the party, of which I am, is to avoid intimate and exclusive connection with any foreign powers.[15]

The case for Madison's views is much simpler. Not needing to establish himself as a genuine American, having been born and raised in Virginia in a prominent family, Madison did not need to make such vehement statements of Americanism as did Hamilton. Nor, however, did he display the Francophilia that many attribute to Thomas Jefferson. As I will show below, his attachment to the French Revolution was the product of a genuine belief in the overwhelmingly positive benefits to the human race of self-government along republican lines. When France gave up its republican experiment in favor of Napoleon, however, he quickly lost his admiration for that country. Like Hamilton, Madison also reached a breaking point regarding events in France.

Writing for the *National Gazette* in 1792, Madison made clear his view that the establishment of government through reason, rather than force, was the greatest accomplishment of the United States, and also of France at that time.

> America has set the example and France has followed it, of charters of power granted by liberty. This revolution in the practice of the world, may, with an honest praise, be pronounced the most triumphant epoch of its history, and the most consoling presage of its happiness.[16]

As I mentioned above, though, once France gave up on republicanism, Madison lost his admiration for France. It became simply another foreign country which the United States needed to deal with as best it could. To Thomas Jefferson he wrote in 1800:

> Such a demonstration of the rectitude & efficacy of popular sentiment, will be the more precious, as the late defection of France has left America the only Theatre on which true liberty can have a fair trial.[17]

Like Hamilton, when it came Madison's turn to take part in Executive branch matters, he also emphasized the desire for the United States to involve itself as little as possible in the affairs of Europe. To Robert Livingston he wrote in 1801:

> It is questionable however whether any leading arrangements by the U. States during the war, even in an eventual form adapted to a state of peace, would be free from the danger of entangling us too much in the present contests & vicisitudes of Europe; or at least of exciting too much the apprehensions of this consequence, among our own Citizens.[18]

Further, his ideas regarding dealing with France and Great Britain once he was Secretary of State are essentially the same as the advice Hamilton provided then-President Washington. I will come back to this later, but I have become convinced the differences between Hamilton and Madison, while real, were not as dramatic as each believed. Both should have followed Lafayette's advice and given each other the benefit of the doubt. In 1802, Madison wrote to Rufus King:

> It is I am persuaded the sincere desire of the people of this Country, and of every department of its Government, to cultivate the most thorough good will, and the most friendly commerce with G. Britain; but I do not believe that they will purchase either by improper sacrifices. . . . I think with you that in our respective stipulations with G.B. & France, it is desirable to have them both so shaped as to avoid as much as possible collisions between them, which might involve the U.S. with one or other of those Nations.[19]

In conclusion, as I stated at the beginning of this chapter, I disagree with Elkins and McKitrick's assessment of the disagreement between Hamilton and Madison as stemming from Hamilton's Anglophilia and Madison's Anglophobia. I can find no clear statement from either that would support that argument. Rather, what I have found is instead a desire by both to establish a clear identity for the nascent United States on the world stage, mainly through staying out of the endless conflicts that characterized European politics, especially at that time.

Hamilton's view of American republicanism stressed independence from all other countries. He wanted to be a part of creating a unique, specifically American, way of acting in the international arena. For him, it was more important for the United States to create an identity separate from either of the "superpowers" of the time, Great Britain and France. Especially in his response to the threat he perceived of the United States becoming a satellite republic of France, as had happened with the Batavian and Helvetic Republics, among others, we see his fear for the continued independence of the United States.

With Madison we see a much less amount of fear for the independence of the United States from France, although he did abandon overt support for France in comparison with Great Britain once Napoleon took control. For Madison, there was much less of a pressing need for the United States to go out of its way to craft a uniquely American approach to dealing with any foreign country. I argue this is due to his, unlike Hamilton, having been a lifelong Virginian and American. He did not have to establish or prove himself worthy of the United States. Madison was much more committed to the idea of republicanism as something that could be successfully established in other countries than he was a supporter of France. He did display a strong antipathy toward Great Britain, but that did not cause him to abandon an idea similar to Hamilton's, that of the United States involving itself as little as possible in the affairs, and especially the wars, of Europe.

NOTES

1. Harold C. Syrett, ed., and Jacob E. Cooke, assoc. ed., *The Papers of Alexander Hamilton*, volume III: 1782–1786 (New York: Columbia University Press, 1962), 291.
2. Ibid, 304.
3. Harold C. Syrett, ed., and Jacob E. Cooke, assoc. ed., *The Papers of Alexander Hamilton*, volume V: June 1788–November 1789 (New York: Columbia University Press, 1962), 425.
4. Harold C. Syrett, ed., and Jacob E. Cooke, assoc. ed., *The Papers of Alexander Hamilton*, volume VII: September 1790–January 1791 (New York: Columbia University Press, 1963), 425–426.
5. Harold C. Syrett, ed., and Jacob E. Cooke, assoc. ed., *The Papers of Alexander Hamilton*, volume VIII: February 1791–July 1791 (New York: Columbia University Press, 1965), 517.
6. Harold C. Syrett, ed., and Jacob E. Cooke, assoc. ed., *The Papers of Alexander Hamilton*, volume XII: July 1792–October 1792 (New York: Columbia University Press, 1967), 229–230.
7. Harold C. Syrett, ed., and Jacob E. Cook, assoc. ed., *The Papers of Alexander Hamilton*, volume XIV: February 1793–June 1793 (New York: Columbia University Press, 1969), 267.
8. Ibid, 503.
9. Harold C. Syrett, ed., and Jacob E. Cooke, assoc. ed., *The Papers of Alexander Hamilton*, volume XVI: February 1794–July 1794 (New York: Columbia University Press, 1972), 266–271.
10. Ibid, 585–586.
11. Harold C. Syrett, ed., *The Papers of Alexander Hamilton*, volume XVIII: January 1795–July 1795 (New York: Columbia University Press, 1973), 374.

12. Harold C. Syrett, ed., *The Papers of Alexander Hamilton*, volume XVIII: January 1795–July 1795 (New York: Columbia University Press, 1973), 453–454.

13. Harold C. Syrett, ed., *The Papers of Alexander Hamilton*, volume XXI: April 1797–July 1798 (New York: Columbia University Press, 1974), 21.

14. Ibid, 287.

15. Ibid, 450–451.

16. Robert A. Rutland, et.al, eds., *The Papers of James Madison*, Volume 14: 6 April 1791–16 March 1793 (Chicago: The University of Chicago Press, 1983), 191.

17. David B. Mattern, et.al, eds., *The Papers of James Madison*, Volume 17: 31 March 1797–3 March 1801, with a supplement 22 January 1778–9 August 1795 (Chicago: The University of Chicago Press, 1991), 377.

18. Robert J. Brugger, et.al, eds. *The Papers of James Madison, Secretary of State Series*, Volume 1: 4 March–31 July 1801 (Charlottesville: University Press of Virginia, 1986), 402.

19. Mary A. Hackett, et.al., eds. *The Papers of James Madison, Secretary of State Series*, Volume 2: 1 August 1801–28 February 1802 (Charlottesville: University Press of Virginia, 1993), 435.

Chapter Four

Hamilton and Madison on Constitutional Interpretation

At the center of Hamilton and Madison's later conflicts, in spite of their earlier collaboration in favor of the Constitution, is precisely their varying interpretations of that document, and what powers each thought it gave the federal government. Focus by others has been thus far on those disagreements, such as over Hamilton's *Report on the Subject of Manufactures* and also whether or not Publius, in the *Federalist Papers*, spoke with two different voices. I myself am going to concentrate my efforts elsewhere, because I am convinced that, for instance, the *Federalist Papers* is in many ways not truly indicative of either Hamilton or Madison's essential points of view, being written to convince potential convention delegates in New York and Virginia to support ratification. Also, the disagreement which emerged over the *Report on the Subject of Manufactures* is exactly the sort of conflict I am trying to explain the reasons for, so I will not include that here.

We will see in the excerpts that follow the very different view Hamilton and Madison had all along regarding the issue of Constitutional interpretation. Even before they worked together on the *Federalist Papers*, they had differences of opinion, and my take on why they never discussed this or any of the other issues I point to is the extreme time constraints they were under while working to write those newspaper articles in support of ratifying the Constitution.

With Hamilton we will see his preference for a loose construction, because for him one simply cannot spell out all the details regarding governmental power in any constitution. He regarded the issue of how to distribute power between the federal and state governments as one of "convenience," rather than of exact definition. For Hamilton, one simply had to set up the government of the United States on a firm foundation, and he thought all one would need thereafter for success would be for elected officials to make "prudent" decisions as to how to administer the nation as a whole.

Madison, however, was very concerned about corruption, about the concentration of too much power in any one set of hands. For him, the boundaries between the various branches of the federal government, and especially between the federal government and the states, needed to be precisely defined in order to prevent overreaching by power-hungry individuals bent on tyranny. He did concede there were ambiguities in the Constitution as written, but he thought those were inevitable, and would be resolved once and for all before long by the accumulation of precedents. That he reacted so strongly to the decisions made during the Washington administration in carrying out policies preferred by Hamilton can be explained by his not wanting "those" precedents to be the way Constitutional ambiguities were resolved.

Hamilton clearly showed the point of view which Madison later came to loathe during his efforts to secure ratification of the Constitution by the state of New York's convention.

> The true principle of government is this—Make the system compleat in its structure; give a perfect proportion and balance to its parts; and the powers you give it will never affect your security. The question then, of the division of powers between the general and state governments, is a question of convenience: It becomes a prudential enquiry, what powers are proper to be reversed to the latter; and this immediately involves another enquiry into the proper objects of the two governments. This is the criterion, by which we shall determine the just distribution of powers.[1]

Corruption was very much on the mind of Madison, whose response to Hamilton's *Report on the Subject of Manufactures* included the argument that basing actions taken by the federal government on the general welfare of the nation would leave the federal government with no limits whatsoever on its powers. But, as we see here, Hamilton was much less concerned with corruption, and clearly felt much more comfortable with the power given to the federal government. Especially, though, note his argument that the division of powers between the states and the federal government is a "question of convenience." This shows the preference we will see in further quotes I will include below that Hamilton had for the federal government over the states.

We see this in Hamilton's desire for more powerful law enforcement in the hands of the federal government. He bemoaned the federal government having to rely on the states to enforce laws. To George Washington he wrote in 1791:

> It is to be lamented that our system is such as still to leave the public peace of the Union at the mercy of each state Government. This is not only the case as it regards direct interferences, but as it regards the *inability* of the National

Government in many particulars to take those direct measures for carrying into execution its views and engagements which exigencies require.[2]

Hamilton was genuinely surprised when Madison began to oppose his policy proposals as Treasury Secretary. He had considered Madison to have the same preference for federal power over state power, but as we have seen this was not really the case. The Constitution was, by 11 out of the 13 states, ratified by 1789. By 1792, Hamilton and Madison's conflict had become apparent to both. To Edward Carrington, Hamilton wrote in 1792:

> I now hold, it was under a full persuasion, that from similarity of thinking, conspiring with personal goodwill, I should have the firm support of Mr. Madison, in the *general course* of my administration. Aware of the intrinsic difficulties of the situation and of the powers of Mr. Madison, I do not believe I should have accepted under a different supposition.[3]

Not only was this a difference of opinion for either man: each considered the ideas the other had as not only mistaken, but dangerous, even bordering on treasonous. I have mentioned this before, and will explore this more fully later, but this is one of the most important aspects of their disagreement. Just like today, neither side in the first political conflicts under the Constitution could consider the other side as legitimate. For both, it was their way of understanding the Constitution, and no other. Also, to Edward Carrington in 1792,

> It was not 'till the last session that I became unequivocally convinced of the following truth—"*That Mr. Madison cooperating with Mr. Jefferson is at the head of a faction decidedly hostile to me and my administration, and actuated by views in my judgment subversive of the principles of good government and dangerous to the union, peace and happiness of the Country.*"[4]

One example of Hamilton's expansive vision for interpreting the Constitution, and thus the powers of the federal government, is his plan to fund, and eventually pay off, the Revolutionary War debt. Hamilton is sometimes portrayed as being in favor of a perpetual debt. That is simply mistaken. His efforts were all focused on paying off that debt, as I have already shown in regard to his support for American neutrality between France and Great Britain. Yet more from his letter to Edward Carrington in 1792,

> Whatever the original merits of the funding system, after having been so solemnly adopted, & after so great a transfer of property under it, what would become of the Government should it be reversed? What of the National Reputation? Upon what system of morality can so atrocious a doctrine be maintained? In me, I confess it excites *indignation & horror*! . . .

> In almost all the questions great & small which have arisen, since the first session of Congress, Mr. Jefferson & Mr. Madison have been found among those who were disposed to narrow the Federal authority. The question of a National Bank is one example.[5]

This quote shows another aspect of Hamilton's concern with giving the federal government more power. He clearly wanted to protect property rights and was afraid of the tendency in the states toward negating such rights through debt relief, paper money, and so on. Thus, he argued in favor of the above-mentioned power to contract for extensive periods of time, which of course would bind subsequent administrations, Congresses, and even later voters.

Hamilton's underlying reason for interpreting the Constitution as he did was his fear that the federal government would not prove strong enough to control the states, which would, in his estimation, eventually lead to a dissolution of the Union, and perhaps even civil war. Because of his desire for a stronger federal government than, say, Madison wanted, some accused him of secretly desiring a return to a monarchical form of government. As Hamilton stated in that letter to Edward Carrington from 1792,

> I am told that serious apprehensions are disseminated in your state as to the existence of a Monarchical party meditating the destruction of State & Republican Government. If it is possible that so absurd an idea can gain ground it is necessary that it should be combatted. I assure you on my *private faith* and *honor* as a Man that there is not in my judgment a shadow of foundation of it. . . .
>
> As to the destruction of State Governments, the *great* and *real* anxiety is to be able to preserve the National from the too potent and counteracting influence of those Governments. As to my own political Creed, I give it to you with the utmost sincerity. I am *affectionately* attached to the Republican theory. I desire *above all things* to see the *equality* of political rights exclusive of all *hereditary* distinction firmly established by a practical demonstration of its being consistent with the order and happiness of society.
>
> As to State Governments, the prevailing byass of my judgment is that if they can be circumscribed within bounds consistent with the preservation of the National Government they will prove useful and salutary. . . .
>
> Hence a disposition on my part towards a liberal construction of the powers of the National Government and to erect every fence to guard it from depredations, which is, in my opinion, consistent with constitutional propriety.[6]

Hamilton and John Adams are often lumped in together as being indicative of Federalist Party thought, but there are in fact many differences between the two, which no doubt contributed to their conflict and eventual break during Adams's term as president. Note Hamilton's argument above in favor of republicanism without hereditary distinctions and in favor of equality of rights. In contrast to how many have interpreted Adams's *A Defence of the Constitutions of Government of the United States of America*, Hamilton here clearly indicates he does not see any need for different orders in society written into the Constitution or law. This is yet another example of the fears both Hamilton and Madison had regarding the other that obscured their similarities.

Another aspect of Hamilton's view of the proper way to interpret the Constitution was his argument that one could never spell out all the details necessary for actually carrying governing into practice. This shows why he favored use of notions such as the "general welfare" as warrant for the policies he wanted to carry out. Madison considered this method dangerous, though, arguing it would lead to no limits whatsoever on what the federal government could do. Regardless, as Hamilton wrote to William Heth in 1791,

> My opinion is that there is and necessarily must be a great number of undefined particulars incident to the general duty of every officer, for the requiring of which no special warrant is to be found in any law. . . .
>
> There is a large chapter of duties *between Executive Officers* which grow out of the Nature of Executive power and which the natural relations of things can alone determine.[7]

Thus, neither the Constitution itself, nor even laws, can have all the details spelled out in advance according to Hamilton. It is up to those who administer both the laws and the Constitution to provide the vast majority of the details. We have seen this Hamiltonian notion carried out in great measure in recent decades by Congress's delegation to the bureaucracy the power to write the actual regulations which provide much of the detail for administering laws.

Overall, Hamilton's method of interpreting the Constitution, and thus his understanding of the way government officials should act, can be accurately characterized by a comment he made to Rufus King in 1798: "You know also how widely different the *business* of Government is from the *speculation* of it, and the energy of the imagination, dealing in general propositions, from that of *execution* in *detail*."[8]

James Madison, on the other hand, had all along some important differences from Hamilton in both his understanding of the importance of the new Constitution, and how it should be put into practice. First of all, he did not display Hamilton's tendency toward a radical break with the approach to governing under the Articles of Confederation, and he certainly did not entertain as much limitation on the powers of the states. To Edmund Randolph, Madison wrote in 1787:

> I think with you that it will be well to retain as much as possible of the old Confederation, tho' I doubt whether it may not be best to work the valuable articles into the new System, instead of engrafting the latter on the former. I am also perfectly of your opinion that in framing a system, no material sacrifices ought to be made to local or temporary prejudices. . . . I hold it for a fundamental point that an individual independence of the States, is utterly irreconcileable with the idea of an aggregate sovereignty.[9]

Even with Madison's most famous attempt to give power to the federal government over the states—that is, his desire for Congress to have a veto on state legislation—he conceived of it not as a replacement of the states by the federal government, but rather a way of providing stability to both governments.

> Let the national Government be armed with a positive & compleat authority in all cases where uniform measures are necessary. As in trade &c. &c. Let it also retain the powers which it now possesses.
>
> Let it have a negative in all cases whatsoever on the Legislative Acts of the States as the K. of G.B. heretofore had. This I conceive to be essential and the least possible abridgement of the State Sovereignties. Without such a defensive power, every positive power that can be given on paper will be unavailing. It will also give internal stability to the States.[10]

Notice Madison's emphasis that the federal government should have "compleat authority" only in cases where "uniform measures are necessary." This is a very different conception of the relationship between the federal and state governments than Hamilton had. Instead of an overwhelming fear of the states, Madison argued that only in certain areas would they need to be restricted, and power instead given to the federal government.

The problem of interpreting the Constitution, and thus how to put it into effect, was on Madison's mind from the very first. He clearly understood that it contained many ambiguities, but he thought those would be removed over time as more and more precedents were established. We can clearly see here the source of Madison's concern with Hamilton's policy proposals, as if these became the precedents on which later practice was to be based, then a way of understanding the Constitution contrary to his own would become the norm. As he stated in 1790, "Among other difficulties, the exposition of the Constitution is frequently a copious source, and must continue so until its meaning on all great points shall have been settled by precedents."[11]

Much more so than Hamilton, Madison all along expressed concerns about the federal government becoming too powerful. However, his primary fear at the beginning of the new federal government was with the power of

Congress, no doubt in part because of the criticisms he had had of the behavior of state legislatures under the Articles of Confederation.

> In truth the Legislative power is of such a nature that it scarcely can be restrained either by the Constitution or by itself. And if the federal Government should lose its proper equilibrium within itself, I am persuaded that the effect will proceed from the Encroachments of the Legislative department.[12]

Madison did express some concern over the power of the state governments, but specifically in regard to civil rights. During the debates in Congress over the then-proposed amendments to the Constitution which became the Bill of Rights, Madison was in favor of extending some of the protections therein to restrict the power of the states. Far before the incorporation of the Bill of Rights through the 14th Amendment by the Supreme Court, Madison was in favor of limiting the states' abilities to violate certain rights. When a fellow member of the House of Representatives moved to strike out "No state shall infringe the equal rights of conscience, nor the freedom of speech, or of the press, nor of the right of trial by jury in criminal cases," Madison responded with this argument, according to the record:

> Mr. Madison Conceived this to be the most valuable amendment on the whole list; if there was any reason to restrain the government of the United States from infringing upon these essential rights, it was equally necessary that they should be secured against the state governments; he thought if they provided against the one, it was as necessary to provide against the others, and was satisfied that it would be equally grateful to the people.[13]

Madison even, in part, agreed with Hamilton's assessment that one could never specify the powers of the federal government in advance through the Constitution. He argued implied powers were inevitable. In response to another House member's proposal to add the word "expressly" just before the word "delegated" in what has become known as the 10th Amendment's phrase where it says, "The powers not delegated by this Constitution, nor prohibited by it to the States, are reserved to the States respectively," Madison's response was,

> Mr. Madison Objected to this amendment, because it was impossible to confine a government to the exercise of express powers. There must necessarily be admitted powers by implication, unless the constitution descended to recount every minutiae. He remembered the word "expressly" had been moved in the convention of Virginia, by the opponents to the ratification, and after full and fair discussion was given up by them, and the system allowed to retain its present form.[14]

When Hamilton began to propose various measures for actually putting the Constitution into practice, however, Madison realized just how different his and his former collaborator's ideas truly were. As I mentioned above with Hamilton, Madison also considered ideas which differed from his own as not only being simply mistaken, but as being subversive and quite possibly even treasonous. It is surprising, as many have noted, just how quickly individuals that knew each other, and had worked together for years and even decades, could so abruptly alter their assessments of each other to conclude that each was up to the worst possible things they could imagine. To Henry Lee, Madison wrote in 1792:

> With respect to the general spirit of the administration you already know how far my ideas square with yours. You know also how extremely offensive some particular measures have been; & I will frankly own, (though the remark is for yourself alone at present) that if they should be followed by the usurpation of power recommended in the report on manufactures, I shall consider the fundamental & characteristic principle of the Govt. as subverted. It will no longer be a Govert. possessing special powers taken from the General Mass, but one possessing the genl. mass with special powers reserved out of it. And this change will take place in defiance of the true & universal construction, & of the sense in which the instrument is known to have been proposed, advocated & ratified.[15]

Here we see clearly Madison's essential disagreement with Hamilton. For Madison, the federal government had only the specific powers given to it by the Constitution, and not the extensive powers proposed by Hamilton. Now, this is clearly in contrast to his earlier statement above that not all the powers of any government could be completely specified in advance. However, I argue Madison's idea regarding implied powers was that the actual powers mentioned in the Constitution could not be completely specified in advance, and thus his disagreement with Hamilton was that powers not specifically mentioned there could not be claimed for the federal government. They needed to be left to, if anywhere, the states. Note also his argument that there was a clear understanding by those who proposed the Constitution regarding what it meant. I will return to this point below.

Madison elaborated on this point in a letter to Edmund Pendleton, also in 1792:

> If Congress can do whatever in their *discretion* can be *done by money*, and will promote the *general welfare*, the Government is no longer a limited one possessing enumerated powers, but an indefinite one subject to particular exceptions.[16]

Madison claimed many times that Hamilton's proposals were in violation of the understanding those who proposed the Constitution had in mind when they created the document, and also that those who accepted the Constitution had in mind as well. This is the main point on which I criticize Madison, as I claim this is a classic example of "begging the question," the well-known logical fallacy. If, as is clear, Hamilton had a rather different understanding of that document, and the powers it gave the new government, how could Madison claim to speak authoritatively for ALL those who had proposed it?

For instance, we know, from his own notes taken at the Constitutional Convention, that the Constitution was itself the result of extensive debate and disagreement. Many, if not most, proposals that were accepted were agreed to only on close votes. It is clear that even the individuals who themselves took part in writing the Constitution had different opinions, and this point is further supported by the sides those who had attended the Constitutional Convention took during the debates of the 1790s. One need look no further for examples than Hamilton and Madison themselves, although they are far from the only ones.

Further, to state that he knew without a doubt how those who had accepted the Constitution had conceived of it is even more subject to criticism. Madison himself knew what every member of every state convention that accepted the Constitution had in mind when voting in favor of it? This is stretching credulity way beyond what can reasonably be expected, as Madison could not have been sure even of the other members of Virginia's ratifying convention, let alone people in other states he never even met.

This weakness in Madison's arguments can be most clearly seen in his *Virginia Resolution*, where he went so far as to claim the final say in interpreting the Constitution for the individual states. Where once he had wanted "to give the new system its proper energy it will be desirable to have it ratified by the authority of the people, and not merely by that of the Legislatures,"[17] he altered his argument to claim that the states, and not the people, were the partners in the social contract that had created the Constitution.

> That this Assembly doth explicitly and peremptorily declare, that it views the powers of the federal government, as resulting from the compact to which the states are parties; as limited by the plain sense and intention of the instrument constituting that compact; as no farther valid than they are authorised by the grants enumerated in that compact, and that in case of a deliberate, palpable and dangerous exercise of other powers not granted by the said compact, the states who are parties thereto have the right, and are in duty bound, to interpose for arresting the progress of the evil, and for maintaining within their respective limits, the authorities, rights and liberties appertaining to them.[18]

In conclusion, I have argued in this chapter that the disagreements which characterized Hamilton and Madison's later careers, after once closely collaborating on the *Federalist Papers*, occurred because each had, all along, distinctly different ideas as to how much power it would be necessary to give to the federal government created by the Constitution they both worked so hard to create and achieve. That they were both surprised by the disagreements they had, once they had secured the Constitution, shows that there never really has been a single way of understanding the role of the Constitution and the federal government in the United States, nor has there been a single way of "defining the republic."

As regards the issue of republicanism, we once again see just how widely different preferences on what a republican government should be like can be held by individuals living at the same time and in the same country. For Hamilton, the difficulty in creating the kind of republic that could survive was what he saw as the centrifugal influence of the states. The states had too much power in his estimation, and people were far more loyal to them than to the United States as a whole. In order for that to succeed, the power of the federal government needed to be increased, very specifically taking power, and citizen loyalty, away from the states. States "could" play a useful role in his vision of the United States, but their influence needed to be as limited as possible. One specific issue he especially feared state influence on was property rights. The states, with their tendencies toward debt relief, paper money, and so on, would undermine the kind of order he saw as necessary for any human society to continue to exist. Thus, the Constitution needed to be interpreted in such ways as to allow the federal government to do the many things he saw as necessary for creating a lasting, successful, powerful, and especially "great" country.

Madison was much less fearful of state power. Yes, he did see a need to give the federal government more power, but he did not see any need for a radical break from the principles of the Articles of Confederation. Greater state power and state sovereignty were realities he had lived with for far longer than Hamilton, so they posed less of a problem in his mind. All the federal government needed were a *few*, well-defined number of powers, in order to assure the success of the federal government, and the United States as a whole. For Madison, the goal was the "least possible abridgement of state sovereignties." As far as the need to resolve Constitutional ambiguities through accumulation of precedent, he preferred a United States where such ambiguities led not to greater power for the federal government, but greater assignment of certain powers and duties to the state governments. For Madison, the United States was far more a collection of individual states, and an entire nation only secondarily. He saw no reason why such a situation could not succeed. Hamilton, on the other hand, was of the exact opposite opinion. In order to succeed, the United States needed to stress its common identity, and *not* its continued existence as a collection of states, where the individual citizen's primary identification was with their state.

NOTES

1. Harold C. Syrett, ed., and Jacob E. Cooke, assoc. ed., *The Papers of Alexander Hamilton*, volume V: June 1788–November 1789 (New York: Columbia University Press, 1962), 97.
2. Harold C. Syrett, ed., and Jacob E. Cooke, assoc. ed., *The Papers of Alexander Hamilton*, volume VIII: February 1791–July 1791 (New York: Columbia University Press, 1965), 269.
3. Harold C. Syrett, ed., and Jacob E. Cooke, assoc. ed., *The Papers of Alexander Hamilton*, volume XI: February 1792–June 1792 (New York: Columbia University Press, 1966), 427.
4. Ibid, 429.
5. Ibid, 437.
6. Ibid, 443.
7. Harold C. Syrett, ed., and Jacob E. Cooke, assoc. ed., *The Papers of Alexander Hamilton*, volume VIII: February 1791–July 1791 (New York: Columbia University Press, 1965), 499–500.
8. Harold C. Syrett, ed., *The Papers of Alexander Hamilton*, volume XXII: July 1798–March 1799 (New York: Columbia University Press, 1975), 192.
9. William T. Hutchinson and William M.E. Rachal, eds., *The Papers of James Madison*, Volume 6: 9 April 1786–24 May 1787 (Chicago: The University of Chicago Press, 1975), 369.
10. Ibid, 370.
11. Charles F. Hobson, et.al, eds., *The Papers of James Madison*, Volume 12: 2 March 1789–20 January 1790, with a supplement 24 October 1775–24 January 1789 (Chicago: The University of Chicago Press, 1979), 250.
12. Ibid, 253.
13. Ibid, 344.
14. Ibid, 346.
15. Robert A. Rutland, et.al, eds., *The Papers of James Madison*, Volume 14: 6 April 1791–16 March 1793 (Chicago: The University of Chicago Press, 1983), 193–194.
16. Ibid, 195–196.
17. William T. Hutchinson and William M.E. Rachal, eds., *The Papers of James Madison*, Volume 6: 9 April 1786–24 May 1787 (Chicago: The University of Chicago Press, 1975), 370.
18. David B. Mattern, et.al, eds., *The Papers of James Madison*, Volume 17: 31 March 1797–3 March 1801, with a supplement 22 January 1778–9 August 1795 (Chicago: The University of Chicago Press, 1991), 189.

Chapter Five

Hamilton and Madison on Religion

Hamilton and Madison did not differ greatly in their opinions on religion, at least as regards the official role of government. Madison, as is well known, opposed much more openly and consistently, any attempt to create or support an official religion for the United States as a whole. He even, as I will show below, wanted to extend the protection of freedom of conscience to apply to the states as well, which would have conflicted with some state laws at the time.

As I have mentioned before, though, my goal in writing this book is to show the underlying differences between Hamilton and Madison, rather than concentrating specifically on the views of either. That sort of work has been done extensively already and does not need to be repeated here. It is the underlying differences which I argue they had all along that led to their eventual political rivalry, and one of the topics on which they differed was religion, albeit not as sharply as in other areas.

Hamilton did display an underlying religious bent all of his life, far less so at the beginning, but nevertheless growing in intensity as he aged. There are few references to religion in Hamilton's early years, but that number increased dramatically toward the end of his life. For Hamilton, the importance of religion stemmed from his conviction that it provided a sense of order and continuity in life that could be found nowhere else. Thus, we will see his quite visceral horrified reaction to the atheism of the French Revolution. That, and the violence I mentioned above in chapter 3, is what turned him away from supporting the French Revolution.

Madison did not display any overt religiosity in any of his writings throughout his life. He did, however, show a consistent and strong belief in the necessity for religious freedom from any official religion, either in Virginia or the United States as a whole. His was an ongoing suspicion of religion, and indeed a great fear of any kind of official religion. Unlike Hamilton,

Madison showed no disapproval of the atheism of the French Revolution. It did not seem to bother him at all. Religion was not necessary for order in society in his view.

As I have read the writings of both, I have found a far greater expressed religiosity, albeit in different forms, throughout the writings of Hamilton than Madison. Like so many people, Hamilton did not overtly express his religious preferences throughout most of his life. Rather, they were part of his underlying understanding of what existence is like and provided him with a sense of meaning and purpose for life itself. This greater religiosity can clearly be seen in the first excerpts from Hamilton's works, a reflection following a hurricane which struck St. Croix, published in *The Royal Danish American Gazette* on September 6, 1772.

> He who gave the winds to blow, and the lightnings to rage—even him have I always loved and served. His precepts have I observed. His commandments have I obeyed—and his perfections have I adored. He will snatch me from ruin. He will exalt me to the fellowship of Angels and Seraphs, and to the fullness of never ending joys. [1]

And:

> Our distressed, helpless condition taught us humility and contempt of ourselves. The horrors of the night, the prospect of an immediate, cruel death—or, as one may say, of being crushed by the Almighty in his anger—filled us with terror.[2]

As I mentioned above, Hamilton was not an overtly religious person throughout most of his life, but one can see again and again the sort of religious references with him that one simply does not find with Madison. The event which does seem to have aroused his greatest amount of reflection on the importance of religion was the French Revolution. Hamilton was horrified by not only the violence and bloodshed which took place, but also by the proclamations of atheism that were prominent amongst those who led the Revolution. In a letter to an unknown correspondent from 1793, Hamilton expressed this negative, indeed visceral, reaction regarding this French undermining of the importance of religion.

> The cause of France is compared with that of America during its late revolution. Would to Heaven that the comparison were just. Would to heaven that we could discern in the Mirror of French affairs, the same humanity, the same decorum, the same gravity, the same order, the same dignity, the same solemnity, which distinguished the course of the American Revolution.[3]

And:

> When I find the doctrines of Atheism openly advanced in the Convention and heared with loud applauses. . . .
>
> I acknowlege, that I am glad to believe, there is no real resemblance between what was the cause of America & what is the cause of France—that the difference is no less great than that between Liberty & Licentiousness.[4]

One sees here Hamilton's connection of religion with social order and reason. Now, as I will argue below, Hamilton did not argue for any sort of official religion on the part of the United States, but rather for an ongoing understanding of, and reference to, religion as part of even official government activity. He was not exclusionary in terms of which specific religion, or at least we have no evidence of that, but rather he equated atheism–that is, a lack of religion, especially Christianity, as part of public life—with chaos and barbarism.

Further evidence of his rejection of the French Revolution comes from an essay he wrote regarding *The War in Europe* in 1796. For Hamilton, Christianity had reduced the level of violence and destruction practiced in early wars, such as those fought by the Roman Empire. For him, French rejection of Christianity was tantamount to a return to Roman barbarism and destruction.

> Every step of the progress of the present war in Europe has been marked with horrors. If the perpetration of them was confined to those who are the acknowleged instruments of despotic Power, it would excite less surprize—but when they are acted by those who profess themselves to be the Champions of the rights of man, they naturally occasion both wonder and regret. . . .
>
> How clearly is it proved [by] all[—]that the praise of a[—]world is justly due to Christianity. War, by the influence of the humane principles of that Religion, had been stripped of half its terrors. The French renounce christianity & they relapse into Barbarism.[5]

Hamilton was far more comfortable with official public events involving religion than Madison. He even went so far to advocate, on more than one occasion, public proclamations and displays by government officials as a means of expressing, or at least trying to influence, the overall sense of the public will. When the French Directory refused to receive Charles Cotesworth Pinckney in 1797, Hamilton wrote to Timothy Pickering what he thought the United States should do.

> It is now ascertained that Mr Pinckney has been refused and with circumstances of indignity. What is to be done? . . .
>
> First. I would appoint a day of humiliation and prayer.[6]

In his speech-writing duties for president Washington, Hamilton also displayed his comfort with a public role for the President in acknowledging and even promoting religiosity among American citizens. Below is a draft he wrote for President Washington in 1795. Note how Hamilton argues the United States should specifically be grateful to God for its favorable situation. For Hamilton, it is God's good will toward the United States that is responsible for the nation's well-being, and thus the nation as a whole should publicly give thanks. However, note the lack of reference to any one kind of religion. It is simply that religious groups are "recommended," not commanded, to take part on a specific day.

> In such a state of things it becomes us in an especial manner as a People, with devout reverence and affectionate gratitude to bow down before the Majesty of the Almighty to acknowlege our numerous obligations to him & to implore under a deep sense of his past goodness a continuance and confirmation of the blessings we experience.
>
> Deeply penetrated with this sentiment I George Washington President of the Ustates do recommend to all religious societies and denominations and to all persons whomsoever within the UStates to set apart and observe Thursday the 19th day of Feby next as a day of public thanksgiving and prayer and on that day to meet together & render their sincere and hearty thanks to the Great Ruler of Nations, for the manifold and signal mercies which distinguish our lot as a Nation;[7]

Even Hamilton's sense of public duty, and I argue even the quest for fame that Douglass Adair and Martin Harvey noted,[8] was in part motivated by his conviction of the absolute importance of religion for organized civil society. Without it, society would fall apart, in his estimation. This is why, to the end of his life, he refrained from intentionally engaging in public behavior which might disqualify him for public service. I say "intentionally" because I am convinced his public letter attacking President John Adams was a blunder he did not fully appreciate the effect of until after he had issued it. Prior to that, though, including during the Quasi-War era, his thoughts explicitly included the need to keep himself available for public service, in part to defend religion. In 1795, he wrote to Robert Troup:

> Because there must be some public fools who sacrifice private to public interest at the certainty of ingratitude and obloquy—because my vanity whispers I ought to be one of those fools and ought to keep myself in a situation the best calculated to render service. . . .
>
> The game to be played may be a most important one. It may be for nothing less than true liberty, property, order, religion and of course heads.[9]

Note how Hamilton equates "true liberty" with not only "property," but also "order, religion," and even "heads." For Hamilton, his lifelong religiosity manifested itself in a conviction that disavowal of religion and religiosity by any nation was a recipe for disaster. Note also his use of "God bless you," something one simply does not find anywhere near as often with Madison.

Even more clear evidence of Hamilton's connection of the French Revolution with chaos because of the violence and rejection of Christianity came during the Quasi-War, and Hamilton's published series of articles entitled, *The Stand*. In number 3, written in 1798, he says,

> In reviewing the disgusting spectacle of the French revolution, it is difficult to avert the eye entirely from those features of it which betray a plan to disorganize the human mind itself, as well as to undermine the venerable pillars that support the edifice of civilized society. The attempt by the rulers of a nation to destroy all religious opinion, and to pervert a whole people to Atheism, is a phenomenon of profligacy reserved to consummate the infamy of the unprincipled reformers of France. The proofs of this terrible design are numerous and convincing.[10]

As I mentioned above, though, even while stressing the importance of religion for civilized society, Hamilton did not show any strong preference for one form of religion over another, at least as far as public policy was concerned. His statements show a marked preference for religiosity among the citizenry, but not any kind of bigotry within the forms of organized religion. While not his own words, a letter written in 1794 from his sister-in-law Angelica Schuyler Church shows a type of open-mindedness toward an otherwise quite unpopular, in England, variant of Christianity, Unitarianism. This, by the way, is a point of agreement between Hamilton and Madison, as we will see below.

> You will have the pleasure to receive this letter by Dr. Priestly, a man dear to virtue and to science. Without the advantage and satisfaction of his acquaintance, I revere him for his works, and take a particular interest that he should be well received in America. That happy country which seems reserved by Providence as an Assylum from the crimes and persecutions which make Europe the pity and disgrace of the age.[11]

Hamilton further emphasized the importance of religion during his service as Inspector General for the Army. At first, he did not think Congress had authorized chaplains, and so wrote the Secretary of War to recommend Congress add them. "There is no provision in the law for Chaplains. I am nevertheless deeply impressed with the importance of divine service among the troops, and have written on the subject to the S of War."[12]

However, later, he did discover that Congress had authorized chaplains, and expressed the importance of filling these positions, not merely because he was simply carrying out the will of Congress, but also because he himself considered provision for religion as important even in the military.

> Application has been made to me on the Subject of Chaplains. I find by recurrence to the laws that four of these characters are provided for. This will furnish one to each brigade. I doubt not you will feel with me strong motives which recommend the speedily going into these appointments.[13]

Hamilton did consider there to be some limits on what kind of religion would be appropriate. In a letter to William S. Smith in 1800, he objected to a potential chaplain candidate due to that individual's "enthusiasm." This is quite similar to his objection to the French Revolution as having gone out of control due to excessive human emotion.

> Enthusiasm is certainly a very good thing, but religious enthusiasm is at least a dangerous instrument. From this, and some other circumstances which have come to my knowledge, I must decline authorizing you to employ the person you mention.[14]

But when George Washington died, in addition to the military honors one would expect an Inspector General would arrange for a former president and commanding general, Hamilton specifically wanted to include the services of a minister. To William North he wrote:

> I enclose to you some regulations relative to the funeral honors to be paid to our departed chief. They will govern generally in the celebration, altho' I have not definitively adopted them.
>
> The ceremonies will be performed in this city on Thursday next, and I should wish them to be performed in New York at the same time. . . . The time is not sufficient for preparing a regular oration, but I should be happy if you could prevail on Doctor Moore or some other Clergyman to deliver a discourse suited to the occasion.[15]

It is in his private life, though, that one can most clearly see his religious sentiments expressed, and just how important they were for his life, even if he did not express them publicly. His letters to his wife, Elizabeth, are especially full of the religious expressions which simply do not occur in similar letters by Madison. In 1797, his father-in-law, Philip Schuyler, had a bout of ill health, and so Hamilton wrote to her: "I pray you, don't alarm yourself for you know how dangerous it will be in your situation and how much it is a duty should his case ever take a worse turn than we now apprehend to arm ourselves with Christian fortitude and resignation."[16]

Also in 1797, when his eldest son Philip also was in bad health, he wrote, "I am arrived here My Dear Eliza in good health but very anxious about my Dear Philip. I pray heaven to restore him and in every event to support you. . . . God bless my beloved and all My Dear Children."[17]

One essential aspect of Hamilton's religious beliefs, already mentioned in regard to the negative influence he believed the French Revolution's emphasis on atheism would have on civilization, is the belief in an afterlife, which he clearly considered provided not only meaning and purpose, but also comfort and consolation, to human life. After one of his wife's sisters died in 1801, he wrote to Elizabeth:

> On Saturday, My Dear Eliza, your sister took leave of her sufferings and friends, I trust, to find repose and happiness in a better country. . . .
>
> I long to come to console and comfort you my darling Betsey. Adieu my sweet angel. Remember the duty of Christian Resignation. Ever Yrs.[18]

This idea of "Christian resignation" was one he used again and again in his correspondence with Elizabeth Hamilton. It is an aspect of his religiosity that appeared well before his son Philip was killed in a duel in 1801 but was clearly evident in his letters to people from whom he had received condolences after Philip's death. To John Dickinson he wrote:

> I was not, My Dear Sir, insensible to the kind attention shewn me by your letter of the 30th. of November last. . . .
>
> Be assured, Sir, that consolation from you on such an occasion was particularly welcome to me, and that I shall always remember it with a grateful sense. The friendship of the wise and good rises in value, in proportion as we learn to form a just estimate of human character and opinion.
>
> That estimate too has a tendency to reconcile us to the departure of those, who are dear to us, from a world, which holds out to virtue many snares, very few supports or recompences.[19]

To Benjamin Rush he wrote, also on March 29, 1802:

> My loss is indeed great. The highest as well as the eldest hope of my family has been taken from me. You estimated him rightly—He was truly a fine youth. But why should I repine? It was the will of heaven; and he is now out of the reach of the seductions and calamities of a world, full of folly, full of vice, full of danger—of least value in proportion as it is best known. I firmly trust also that he has safely reached the haven of eternal repose and felicity.[20]

Among those few expressions of his religious beliefs that we have in his papers to anyone other than immediate family, is his letter to Martha Washington after George Washington's death.

> I did not think it proper, Madam, to intrude amidst the first effusions of your grief. . . . Satisfied that you cannot receive consolation, I will attempt to offer none. Resignation to the will of Heaven, which the practice of your life ensures, can alone alleviate the sufferings of so heart-rending an affliction.[21]

Even when faced with possible death, Hamilton expressed how he intended to behave based on his Christian beliefs. Now, the expressions he made did show a difference in the preparations he made and the sentiments he recorded between his upcoming duel with Aaron Burr and the earlier preparations he had made for other possible duels. One of Hamilton's flaws, perhaps his greatest, was his extraordinary concern for his personal honor. It is only a guess to say it was based on his family background (parents of uncertain marriage status), and lack of established family connections, but nevertheless the concern was there. We have several incidents recorded amongst his own papers where he felt the possibility of fighting a duel was his only choice. However, it is only with the last, his duel with Burr, that we have any strong religious sentiments tied directly to the upcoming event.

In a statement regarding the upcoming "interview," Hamilton wrote he was not eager to participate, due to the possibility of harming another human being, which he deplored due to his Christian beliefs. "My religious and moral principles are strongly opposed to the practice of Duelling, and it would even give me pain to be obliged to shed the blood of a fellow creature in a private combat forbidden by the laws."[22]

To Elizabeth Hamilton he wrote:

> The consolations of Religion, my beloved, can alone support you; and these you have a right to enjoy. Fly to the bosom of your God and be comforted. With my last idea; I shall cherish the sweet hope of meeting you in a better world.[23]

When, after the duel, Hamilton realized he was a dying man, his thoughts were of making a final expression of his religious beliefs. As is well known, he requested two different clergymen to give him communion as a final statement regarding his beliefs. I am including Benjamin Moore's statement to William Coleman so as to provide documentation of Hamilton's deep-seated beliefs. Much as the statement of a dying person is taken quite seriously in the law, Hamilton's intention at this point of his life shows the intensity of his beliefs.

> Upon my entering the room and approaching his bed, with the utmost calmness and composure he said, "My dear Sir, you perceive my unfortunate situation, and no doubt have been made acquainted with the circumstances which led to it. It is my desire to receive the communion at your hands. I hope you will not conceive there is any impropriety in my request." He added, "It has for some time

past been the wish of my heart, and it was my intention to take an early opportunity of uniting myself to the church, by the reception of that holy ordinance."[24]

So, all well and good. Hamilton had an underlying sense of religion that we can document from his earliest to his last days. He was convinced not only of the importance of religion in his own life, but also for the good of civilization as a whole. How did this affect his views of what the United States should be and become? This we can clearly see in his plan, expressed to James Bayard in 1802, for a "Christian Constitutional Society," in response to the threat he perceived of an American version of French Jacobinism and atheism.

> Let an Association be formed to be denominated, "The Christian Constitutional Society." It's objects to be
> 1st The support of the Christian Religion.
> 2nd The support of the Constitution of the United States. [25]

Notice the means mentioned by Hamilton. This is not an attempt to impose a nationwide, official church or religion on all citizens. Nor is it an attempt to make laws for the mind, something we will see Madison was concerned with below. Rather, it is an attempt to influence the population at large from a Christian-based point of view. Not only does it include dissemination of ideas Hamilton would have found acceptable, but it also includes charitable efforts to help the less fortunate. The goal here is to inculcate in the minds of the population an association between the Christian religion and not only good order, but also good acts.

What Madison would have thought of all this we do not know. As I have mentioned before, and will document below, his concerns were with preventing the imposition of any one form of religion, Christian or otherwise, on those who did not accept or want it. This is understandable due to his growing up in Virginia, with its established, tax-supported, church. I am saying nothing that has not already been well-documented before when I note that Madison loathed having an established church. It was a threat not only to freedom of thought, but political freedom as well. To William Bradford he wrote in 1774:

> If the Church of England had been the established and general Religion in all the Northern Colonies as it has been among us here and uninterrupted tranquility had prevailed throughout the Continent, It is clear to me that slavery and Subjection might and would have been gradually insinuated among us. Union of Religious Sentiments begets a surprizing confidence and Ecclesiastical Establishments tend to great ignorance and Corruption all of which facilitate the Execution of mischevious Projects.[26]

Not only did an established church prevent freedom of thought and political freedom, it also had a negative effect on the people themselves, in Madison's estimation. The lethargy it created in personal matters manifested itself in ethical and moral decline, not the positive effects those, such as Patrick Henry, argued having an established church would create.

> That diabolical Hell conceived principle of persecution rages among some and to their eternal Infamy the Clergy can furnish their Quota of Imps for such business. This vexes me the most of any thing whatever.[27]

In fact, Madison argued not imposing any one type of religion on the population through an established church would create the positive effects proponents of an established church wanted. Also, to William Bradford, who was from Pennsylvania, a state with no one established religion, he wrote in 1774:

> You are happy in dwelling in a Land where those inestimable privileges are fully enjoyed and the public has long felt the good effects of their religious as well as Civil Liberty. . . . Religious bondage shackles and debilitates the mind and unfits it for every noble enterprize every expanded prospect.[28]

Madison's *A Memorial and Remonstrance* contains his main thoughts and points regarding how he envisioned the United States should be regarding religion. His thought, as I have mentioned, centered on religious freedom, but there are multiple points he raises in that document that deserve especial attention and comment.

> Because we hold it for a fundamental and undeniable truth, "that Religion or the duty which we owe to our Creator and the manner of discharging it, can be directed only by reason and conviction, not by force or violence."[29]

The American Revolution was fought, in part, to defend the "unalienable rights" of the colonists. Madison here adds to Jefferson's "Life, Liberty and the Pursuit of Happiness" freedom of religion. This Lockean estimation of religion as among the rights which are unalienable because doing so would negate the very reason for the existence of government, is in this instance Madison's addition to Locke's "Life, Liberty and Property" formulation for the basis of organized society.

> It is unalienable, because the opinions of men, depending only on the evidence contemplated by their own minds cannot follow the dictates of other men:[30]

The right to freely choose what religion to follow and support is a duty which exists even before any government has been created, one which every human owes to the Creator. Madison here argues that governments that try to establish any one religion, and enforce recognition of it by the citizenry, are in fact trespassing on something owed to God, and not to any human government.

> We maintain therefore that in matters of Religion, no mans right is abridged by the institution of Civil Society and that Religion is wholly exempt from its cognizance[31]

By definition, then, religion is beyond the ability of government to legislate. Government cannot legislate in matters concerning God or religion, because those are superior to government.

> The preservation of a free Government requires not merely, that the metes and bounds which separate each department of power be invariably maintained; but more especially that neither of them be suffered to overleap the great Barrier which defends the rights of the people.[32]

Just as preservation of freedom and rights necessitates the division of power between the branches of government, so it depends on a division of power between the government and the rights of the people. Further, any attempt by government to legislate on religion turns the individuals responsible into dictators.

> Who does not see that the same authority which can establish Christianity, in exclusion of all other Religions, may establish with the same ease any particular sect of Christians, in exclusion of all other Sects?[33]

Hearkening back to the Revolution again, and the reasons why Americans chose to fight, Madison compares this *Remonstrance* with the efforts to respond to what the colonists considered British threats to their rights. Just as the colonists had objected to British efforts, so those who object to this attempt to establish a church are following the same path.

> Whilst we assert for ourselves a freedom to embrace, to profess and to observe the Religion which we believe to be of divine origin, we cannot deny an equal freedom to those whose minds have not yet yielded to the evidence which has convinced us.[34]

The only one who need be concerned with enforcing "correct" religious belief is God, not any government or government official, and in fact is an example of government intruding on matters only God can adequately judge.

> Because the Bill implies either that the Civil Magistrate is a competent Judge of Religious Truth; or that he may employ Religion as an engine of Civil policy.[35]

Further, Christianity specifically has always considered itself as "not of this world," and separate from secular authorities. So, having an established, government-approved and supported church contradicts the faith of those who do profess it, and creates the impression amongst those who do not that Christianity would not survive without official sanction.

> Because the establishment proposed by the Bill is not requisite for the support of the Christian Religion. To say that it is, is a contradiction to the Christian Religion itself, for every page of it disavows a dependence on the powers of this world.[36]

Madison also calls attention to the history of official churches. They do not have a good track record as regards individual rights. In fact, they have often been the sources of oppression. Not only that, once again Madison argues they have a negative effect on individual ethics and morality, not the positive effects argued for by supporters of official religions.

> Because experience witnesseth that ecclesiastical establishments, instead of maintaining the purity and efficacy of Religion, have had a contrary operation.[37]

One of the enticements to emigrate to Virginia has been, Madison argues, the freedom to worship as one chose. If that is taken away, Virginia will lose that attractiveness to potential immigrants, and will also tend to drive away people who currently do live in Virginia, thus weakening the state in each way.

> Because the proposed establishment is a departure from that generous policy, which, offering an Asylum to the persecuted and oppressed of every Nation and Religion, promised a lustre to our country, and an accession to the number of its citizens.[38]

Madison argues religious conflicts all too easily become violent, and so every effort needs to be made to avoid them, especially by not establishing one religion as official, because that would by definition put all the others in a subservient situation.

> Because it will destroy that moderation and harmony which the forbearance of our laws to intermeddle with Religion has produced among its several sects.[39]

He also argues laws which are unpopular and unacceptable to large groups of citizens, even if they do not constitute a majority of the population, weaken overall respect for laws in general. Such a law would be resented by many, who would then learn to treat other laws with contempt as well. This would lead to contempt for government itself and create far more difficulty than it is worth.

> Because attempts to enforce by legal sanctions, acts obnoxious to so great a proportion of Citizens, tend to enervate the laws in general, and to slacken the bands of Society.[40]

Finally, a violation of the right of freedom of religion is a violation of all other rights, at least in essence. If the right to a free choice regarding religion can be violated, what cannot? All rights must be protected, lest any of them be transgressed. Just as it is necessary to protect the freedom of speech, freedom of the press, and other liberties, so it is necessary to protect freedom of religion.

> Because finally, "the equal right of every citizen to the free exercise of his Religion according to the dictates of conscience" is held by the same tenure with all our other rights.[41]

Madison noted in a letter to Thomas Jefferson, in which he enclosed the *Remonstrance*, that clergy opposition to the proposed establishment had already occurred among those whose religion was not made official. Madison approved of this, not because of the envy and fear it showed between the sects, but rather because it was a convenient and effective means of preventing passage of the bill.

> The mutual hatred of these sects has been much inflamed by the late act incorporating the latter. *I am far from* being *sorry for it* as *a coalition between them* could *alone endanger our religious rights* and a tendency to *such an event had been suspected.*[42]

During the debate over ratifying the Constitution in Virginia's ratifying convention, Madison argued that the lack of a bill of rights specifically enumerating the freedom of religion was not necessary, ironically in response to criticism regarding such a lack from Patrick Henry, who had been a supporter of the establishment bill Madison had opposed. What good would a "Bill of Rights" do against a majority, Madison argued. What was needed was what the United States already had, a multiplicity of different religions and sects, each of whom could be counted upon to oppose any efforts to establish one or another of them as official.

> Happily for the states, they enjoy the utmost freedom of religion. This freedom arises from that multiplicity of sects, which pervades America, and which is the best and only security for religious liberty in any society. For where there

> is such a variety of sects, there cannot be a majority of any one sect to oppress and persecute the rest. Fortunately for this commonwealth, a majority of the people are decidely against any exclusive establishment—I believe it to be so in the other states. There is not a shadow of right in the general government to intermeddle with religion.[43]

Now, of course, Madison did eventually see the need to add a Bill of Rights to the Constitution and was instrumental in their writing and passage. Further, we have several of his comments in the House of Representatives by which to gauge his understanding of, most importantly on the subject of religion, the 1st Amendment. "Mr. Madison said he apprehended the meaning of the words to be, that congress should not establish a religion, and enforce the legal observation of it by law, nor compel men to worship God in any manner contrary to their conscience."[44]

In addition to protection from the federal government for religious freedom, Madison wanted state governments to be similarly prohibited. As the minutes of the House of Representatives from August 17, 1789, note,

> Tucker moved to strike out, "No state shall infringe the equal rights of conscience, nor the freedom of speech, or of the press, nor of the right of trial by jury in criminal cases."
>
> Mr. Madison Conceived this to be the most valuable amendment on the whole list; if there was any reason to restrain the government of the United States from infringing upon these essential rights, it was equally necessary that they should be secured against the state governments; he thought that if they provided against the one, it was as necessary to provide against the other, and was satisfied that it would be equally grateful to the people.[45]

Madison was, like Hamilton, accepting of other religions besides Protestant Christianity, and not hostile to them. Just as Hamilton welcomed Unitarians, so did Madison. As he wrote to George Nicholas in 1793,

> His partiality to our Country makes him anxious to settle in it: and as he is not likely to find a Religious Society with which he could connect himself as a Minister professing the Unitarian System taught by Priestly & others, he wishes to see if there be any prospect of his establishing himself an an instructor of youth in classical knowledge and other branches of liberal education; for which he is probably well qualified.[46]

Further, he was also accepting of Roman Catholics, and saw them as no threat to republican government. In a speech in the House of Representatives on January 1, 1795, he is noted as saying,

> He did not approve the ridicule attempted to be thrown out on the Roman Catholics. In their religion, there was nothing inconsistent with the purest republicanism. . . . Americans had no right to ridicule Catholics. They had, many of them, proved good citizens, during the revolution.[47]

So, as regards religion, how do Hamilton and Madison compare? I do not see any overt conflict in the writings we have, although it does appear possible that Hamilton's "Christian Constitutional Society" idea might have, had he lived longer, and had such idea even taken off, been the source of potential conflict. Hamilton did not specifically call for any official recognition of Christianity, though, but rather simply for the dissemination of ideas which would no doubt have supported a religious, rather than an atheistic, approach to public life.

Both were, as I have noted, accepting of religious groups outside of the majority Protestant sects. What differentiates the two is the much greater religious sense that Hamilton had throughout his life, and his much greater negative response to the French Revolution because of its disavowal of religion. Madison did not turn against France until after Napoleon had taken power, and thus turned France away from the republican experiment.

Hamilton, while not showing any preference for an official church of any kind, nevertheless believed strongly, at least toward the end of his life, that religion was an absolute necessity for the success of the American republic. He saw no trouble at all having religion in government, such as military chaplains, and official calls for days of religious expression by even the president himself. Too much religious "enthusiasm" was a bad thing, though, and he did not show any support for nonstandard, or extreme, varieties of religion. Religion was an essential support of order, continuity, meaning and purpose for all humans, and even a republic such as the United States needed to have religion as part of its public life, although an official church was never mentioned as essential by him.

Madison was convinced religion was best left up to the individual sects, both in terms of the success of the United States as a whole, and also as a means of keeping religion from having too much influence in public life. He had, after all, grown up in a colony, later state, which had had an official religion, and so was far more concerned with the negative effects he saw official religions as having. For Madison, the danger was *not* in a lack of religion in public life, as with Hamilton, but rather one of official religions as a barrier to political freedom, and thus the success of a republic built on freedom. Madison wanted religion left up to the reason and conscience of each individual and saw no reason to have it included in official public life. It could only be a danger to the success of the American republic, and not an asset, again in stark contrast to Hamilton.

NOTES

1. Harold C. Syrett, ed., and Jacob E. Cooke, assoc. ed., *The Papers of Alexander Hamilton*, volume I: 1768–1778 (New York: Columbia University Press, 1961), 34–39.

2. Ibid, 34–39.

3. Harold C. Syrett, ed., and Jacob E. Cooke, assoc. ed., *The Papers of Alexander Hamilton*, volume XIV: February 1793–June 1793 (New York: Columbia University Press, 1969), 473–476.

4. Ibid, 473–476.

5. Harold C. Syrett, ed., *The Papers of Alexander Hamilton*, volume XX: January 1796–March 1797 (New York: Columbia University Press, 1974), 339–340.

6. Ibid, 545.

7. Harold C. Syrett, ed., and Jacob E. Cooke, assoc. ed., *The Papers of Alexander Hamilton*, volume XVIII: January 1795–July 1795 (New York: Columbia University Press, 1973), 2–3.

8. Douglass Adair and Martin Harvey, "Was Alexander Hamilton a Christian Statesman?" *The William and Mary Quarterly*, Third Series 12, No. 2 (1955), 308–329.

9. Harold C. Syrett, ed., and Jacob E. Cooke, assoc. ed., *The Papers of Alexander Hamilton*, volume XVIII: January 1795–July 1795 (New York: Columbia University Press, 1973), 328–329.

10. Harold C. Syrett, ed., *The Papers of Alexander Hamilton*, volume XXI: April 1797–July 1798 (New York: Columbia University Press, 1974), 402.

11. Harold C. Syrett, ed., and Jacob E. Cooke, assoc. ed., *The Papers of Alexander Hamilton*, volume XVI: February 1794–July 1794 (New York: Columbia University Press, 1972), 225.

12. Harold C. Syrett, ed., *The Papers of Alexander Hamilton*, volume XXIV: November 1799–June 1800 (New York: Columbia University Press, 1976), 37–38.

13. Ibid, 155–156.

14. Ibid, 320–321.

15. Ibid, 114–115.

16. Harold C. Syrett, ed., *The Papers of Alexander Hamilton*, volume XXI: April 1797– July 1798 (New York: Columbia University Press, 1974), 51.

17. Ibid, 294–295.

18. Harold C. Syrett, ed., *The Papers of Alexander Hamilton*, volume XXV: July 1800–April 1802 (New York: Columbia University Press, 1977), 348–349.

19. Ibid, 583.

20. Ibid, 583–584.

21. Harold C. Syrett, ed., *The Papers of Alexander Hamilton*, volume XXIV: November 1799–June 1800 (New York: Columbia University Press, 1976), 184–185.

22. Harold C. Syrett, ed., *The Papers of Alexander Hamilton*, volume XXVI: May 1, 1802–October 23, 1804, Additional Documents 1774–1799, Addenda and Errata (New York: Columbia University Press, 1979), 278.

23. Ibid, 293.

24. Ibid, 314–317.

25. Harold C. Syrett, ed., *The Papers of Alexander Hamilton*, volume XXV: July 1800–April 1802 (New York: Columbia University Press, 1977), 606–608.

26. William T. Hutchinson, and William M.E. Rachal, eds., *The Papers of James Madison*, Volume 1: 16 March 1751–16 December 1779 (Chicago: The University of Chicago Press, 1962), 105.

27. Ibid, 106.

28. Ibid, 112–113.

29. Robert A. Rutland, et.al, eds., *The Papers of James Madison*, Volume 8: 10 March 1784–28 March 1786 (Chicago: The University of Chicago Press, 1973), 299.

30. Ibid.

31. Ibid.

32. Ibid, 299–300.

33. Ibid, 300.

34. Ibid.

35. Ibid, 301.

36. Ibid.

37. Ibid.

38. Ibid, 302.

39. Ibid, 302–303.

40. Ibid, 303.

41. Ibid, 304.

42. Ibid, 345.

43. Robert A. Rutland, et.al, eds., *The Papers of James Madison*, Volume 11: 7 March 1788–1 March 1789 (Chicago: The University of Chicago Press, 1977), 130–131.

44. Charles F. Hobson, et.al, eds., *The Papers of James Madison*, Volume 12: 2 March 1789–20 January 1790, with a supplement 24 October 1775–24 January 1789 (Chicago: The University of Chicago Press, 1979), 339.

45. Ibid, 344.

46. Thomas A. Mason, et.al, eds., *The Papers of James Madison*, Volume 15: 24 March 1793–20 April 1795 (Chicago: The University of Chicago Press, 1985), 139–140.

47. Ibid, 432–433.

Chapter Six

Hamilton on the Federal Government's Role in the Economy

Of all the areas on which Hamilton and Madison came into conflict beginning in the 1790s, the issue of whether, and how much, the federal government should involve itself in the economy is one of the clearer examples of how, as I argue, they had underlying differences of opinion all along. Both Hamilton and Madison displayed their later preferences regarding economic involvement well before the Constitution was in place, as I will document below. I am convinced the differences we will see regarding the economy were issues they simply did not discuss before their eventual break.

For Hamilton, we will see it is not only appropriate, but indeed essential, that specifically the federal government take an active role in the economy. There is for him a danger in not having the federal government involve itself in the economy, as only the federal government can take the actions he sees as necessary for the survival and success of the United States. A strictly free market is neither desirable nor possible for Hamilton, as individual initiative will just not lead to the successful economy that can provide the people of the United States with the wealth that will convince them to continue to support the American republican experiment.

I mentioned in chapter 4 that I would not discuss Hamilton's *Report on the Subject of Manufactures* as part of the issue of Constitutional interpretation, but such a discussion is of course essential when dealing with the question of the economy. So, I will include that below, but the differences of opinion between Hamilton and Madison are evident before that document came to light. Well before the Constitution was written, Hamilton argued for the appropriateness, indeed necessity, of government involvement in the economy through regulation. In *The Continentalist* No. V, from 1782, he wrote:

> The vesting Congress with the power of regulating trade ought to have been a principal object of the confederation for a variety of reasons. . . . Commerce, like other things, has its fixed principles, according to which it must be regulated.[1]

Clearly this is not an argument in favor of laissez faire, nor even of the much more free market options preferred by Adam Smith. Just as with government, Hamilton argues there are laws which govern the economy. Also, Hamilton did not want to leave the issue of regulation to the state governments, as that was precisely one of the main problems he saw with the Articles of Confederation. The United States needs specific federal government involvement in the economy in order to achieve the best results. The states are only parts of a whole.

> Perhaps it may be thought, that the power of regulation will be left placed in the governments of the several states, and that a general superintendence is unnecessary. If the states had distinct interests, were unconnected with each other . . . but as they are parts of a whole with a common interest in trade, as in other things, there ought to be a common direction in that as in all other matters.[2]

Hamilton does agree with Madison that the most convenient form of taxation is tariffs. However, he shows he was consistent throughout his political life in the United States in having an overriding preference for the United States' well-being as a whole, rather than that of any one state. For him, the states are rather like jealous siblings, afraid someone will get more than they. Hamilton's goals for the United States did include "greatness," one of his departures from classical republican thought, and a "great" people thinks beyond the narrow self-interest of any one sector to reach for more than mere survival or mediocrity. I am convinced this was the result of his not growing up in one state or another, but rather the Caribbean.

> We seem not to reflect, that in human society, there is scarcely any plan, however salutary to the whole and to every part, by the share, each has in the common prosperity, but in one way, or another, and under particular circumstances, will operate more to the benefit of some parts, than of others. Unless we can overcome this narrow disposition and learn to estimate measures, by their general tendency, we shall never be a great or a happy people, if we remain a people at all.[3]

Hamilton argued there were dangers inherent in a lack of federal government oversight of the economy. There would be a lack of money that might otherwise be available. The government itself would not have the power and revenue necessary for any government to exist, and this would be an ongoing threat to the continuation of the Union between the states. Overall, he argued that government oversight of the economy would lead to increased prosperity for all Americans.

> Let us see what will be the consequences of not authorising the Fœderal Government to regulate the trade of these states.
>
> Besides the want of revenue and of power, besides the immediate risk to our independence, the danger of all the future evils of a precarious union, besides the deficiency of a wholesome concert and provident superintendence to advance the general prosperity of trade, the direct consequence will be, that the landed interest and the labouring poor will in the first place fall a sacrifice to the trading interest, and the whole eventually to a bad system of policy, made necessary by the want of such regulating power.[4]

Further, the people of the United States need protection which only the federal government can provide, specifically the poor and those whose primary wealth consists in land. They need protection, Hamilton argued, precisely from "the trading interest." As we will see below, this is quite similar to a point Madison raised as well. Hamilton saw a need for regulation to protect workers and farmers. Overall, a lack of regulation would, in Hamilton's estimation, have negative effects for the United States as a whole. The states are not even mentioned as possible sources of this protection. Only the federal government can do this, across the entirety of the United States.

> The influence of these evils will be, to render landed property fluctuating and less valuable, to oppress the poor by raising the prices of necessaries, to injure commerce by encouraging the consumption of foreign luxuries, by encreasing the value of labor, by lessening the quantity of home productions, enhancing their prices at foreign markets, of course, obstructing their sale and enabling other nations to supplant us.[5]

However, government oversight of the economy, especially through taxation, requires keeping in mind the good of the entirety of society, and not privileging any one or more sector to the detriment of the rest. Taxation needs to be apportioned well, in order to create good order. Also, anyone who thinks taxation can be avoided simply does not, according to Hamilton, have a good understanding of the realities of human life. Human life requires government, government requires well-compensated people to administer it, and administration requires revenue, which can only be obtained through taxation. Taxation will bring benefits, though, such as increased safety from attack, both at home from other countries, and also increased safety abroad for the United States' trade with foreign lands. Both are absolutely necessary in Hamilton's estimation, and the need for both will never cease.

> The great art is to distribute the public burthens well and not suffer them, either first, or last, to fall too heavily upon parts of the community; else distress and disorder must ensue. A shock given to any part of the political machine vibrates through the whole.[6]

Hamilton even argued that there should be differences in taxation according to overall wealth, something which is still contentious even today. Nevertheless, the idea does appear in his sentiments regarding "the rich" again and again throughout his life. "The rich must be made to pay for their luxuries; which is the only proper way of taxing their superior wealth."[7]

As always with Hamilton, he expressed his concern for strengthening and preserving the Union. He argued again and again for the need to support and emphasize the importance of the federal government. For Hamilton, the danger was *not* an overly powerful federal government, but rather the centrifugal effects of, in his estimation, overly powerful states. The United States needs to create a sense of national loyalty, *not* state-centered loyalties. Greatness, including safety and prosperity, is possible for Hamilton *only* in the Union, and not in smaller republics, such as individual states, or the smaller confederations others had called for the United States to split into in the years prior to ratification of the Constitution. Only a federal government with sufficient power can achieve these worthwhile ends, which Hamilton argues will benefit everyone across the United States.

> The reason of allowing Congress to appoint its own officers of the customs, collectors of taxes, and military officers of every rank, is to create in the interior of each state a mass of influence in favour of the Fœderal Government.[8]

While not an official part of his visions for the federal government itself, Hamilton did help propose a "manufacturing society." For him, increasing manufacturing in the United States was central to his goals of American independence and greatness. Improving the diversity of occupations and kinds of business would also help pay off the Public Debt, which all too often he has been erroneously accused of wanting to make permanent. For Madison, however, manufacturing was an evil he expected to eventually make its way to the United States, but he feared and dreaded it as a threat to republican simplicity and virtue. Hamilton displayed no such apprehensions, though. To William Duer he wrote in 1791:

> I send you herewith a plan for a manufacturing Society in conformity to the Ideas we have several times conversed about. . . .
>
> The more I have considered the thing, the more I feel persuaded that it will equally promote the Interest of the adventurers & of the public and will have an excellent effect on the Debt.[9]

In the *Prospectus of the Society for Establishing Useful Manufactures*, Hamilton stressed the need for the United States to focus on prosperity. While not necessarily opposed to virtue, prosperity was for Hamilton vital for the continued existence of the United States. For political perfection to be attained in the United States, Hamilton argued wealth was necessary, and the United States needed manufacturing in order to acquire wealth. He did mention the usefulness, at the time, of the public debt as a resource, a source of capital, to help in expanding and diversifying the economy through encouraging manufacturing.

> The establishment of Manufactures in the United States when maturely considered will be found to be of the highest importance to their prosperity. . . .
>
> The last objection disappears in the eye of those who are aware how much may be done by a proper application of the public Debt. Here is the resource which has been hitherto wanted.[10]

Of all of Hamilton's thoughts and works on economic matters, his massive *Report on the Subject of Manufactures* is the most important, not only because of the breadth of subjects he covers, but also because it is his single most comprehensive statement regarding what he thought was right for the United States. That it provoked yet another conflict with Madison shows us again the differences in expectations between these two vital Founders.

From the beginning of the report, he stresses several points he considers to be reasons why the United States needs to add manufacturing to what was then an overwhelmingly agricultural economy. Again, the goal behind his policy proposals is the continued independence of the United States through increasing its overall power by adding manufacturing to its economy. Having an economy based primarily on agricultural exports to other countries is a weakness, and the United States should increase its domestic market in order to improve its economy.

Manufacturing is a source of outlets for agricultural products, so the two are not incompatible. Agriculture is preeminent, of course, but there is no reason not to add manufacturing. Hamilton's statements regarding agriculture do show the same republican virtue emphasis that Madison stressed in his arguments, but for Hamilton, manufacturing is not the threat Madison feared. Manufacturing is, for Hamilton, just as productive as agriculture, which differentiated Hamilton from many other thinkers of his time.

There is a need for society to have, as Hamilton argues, a proper division of labor in order to have the best possible economy. "It has justly been observed, that there is scarcely any thing of greater moment in the œconomy of a nation, than the proper division of labour."[11] Having manufacturing will help the United States in another way, through attracting immigrants. Increasing the number of occupations is beneficial, because it leads to greater innovation throughout society. However, the United States does need to take care to be self-sufficient as regards its food supply, and also its raw materials used in the manufacturing sector Hamilton wants.

Reliance solely on agriculture, though, has been a disadvantage for the United States thus far, and will only continue to be so if manufacturing is not added. Demand for agricultural products overseas is not reliable and is thus not a good source of money which can be relied upon at all times. Especially given how fast the United States population is growing, if it continues to rely solely on agriculture, that vast increase of people, all working in farming, will only lead to an ever greater supply, which will eventually lead to an over-abundance. Manufacturing will help ease that by providing an outlet other than exports of American farm products.

Hamilton further argues manufacturing will actually help give farmers an incentive to improve their lands, since they will have to find ways to deal with the movement of workers from farming to industry. Manufacturing also leads to different, new, industries, such as mining, thus providing even more diversification and strength to the economy overall.

Hamilton and Madison did both, at various points in their careers, mention a preference for free trade among all nations. However, both also noted that other countries, such as Great Britain, did not follow that practice, so both argued that the United States could not rely on free trade at that time. The United States was simply not on equal terms with any country in Europe at that point.

> If the system of perfect liberty to industry and commerce were the prevailing system of nations—the arguments which dissuade a country in the predicament of the United States, from the zealous pursuits of manufactures would doubtless have great force. . . .
>
> But the system which has been mentioned, is far from characterising the general policy of Nations.[12]

Hamilton further mentions an issue which would continue to be controversial throughout most of the history of the United States, that of "internal improvements," but in a way which shows he completely approved of them. Internal improvements, like manufacturing, would in his estimation, only make things better for Americans. He also argued the sooner the United States was independent of Europe economically, the better.

Hamilton did show an influence from classical republican thought in his estimation that even if manufacturing is encouraged by government, most people will nevertheless still desire to be farmers, due to the independence of that occupation which was taken for granted at that time.

Overall, for Hamilton there is an ongoing need for government involvement in the economy. Laissez-faire is simply not possible in his view of human nature. Government involvement is necessary for the improvement of society, as, for instance, habit and imitation all too often lead to a fear of innovation. People will often simply not risk their own resources in order to make improvements, and so government needs to step in and provide the source of innovation. This is for Hamilton a never-ending positive role for government, as a means of improving the economy over time. Government involvement leads to risk taking that would not otherwise occur.

Plus, the United States had an especially strong need for government at its beginning, because it needed to overcome already established industries in other countries. Nascent industries in the United States simply could not effectively compete with much more established manufacturers elsewhere, if for no other reason than the support those industries already received from their own governments. Thus, the United States needed to do the same. Government support of manufacturing in other countries was, in Hamilton's estimation, the single greatest barrier to growth of industry in the United States.

Individual initiative, while lauded by Hamilton, was for the reasons he mentioned above, just not enough, given the particular circumstances the United States found itself in at the time he submitted his report to Congress. The only resource available was for the United States to mimic the business-encouraging behavior of Europeans. In a time of primary reliance on specie for use as money, and given its general scarcity in the United States, what options were available to provide the capital essential for the creation and maintenance of a manufacturing economy? The public debt, specifically the securities of the United States, can be used as money, due to the reliable value Hamilton argued such securities would have in the minds of those exchanging them.

> Public Funds answer the purpose of Capital, from the estimation in which they are usually held by Monied men; and consequently from the Ease and dispatch with which they can be turned into money.[13]

Hamilton emphasized the "utility" of making such use of the debt. However, again in contrast to a common misunderstanding of Hamilton, he did not argue that the more debt, existing in perpetuity, the better. This was for him only a temporary measure, to provide a means by which greater economic exchange across the United States could be encouraged in the short term. He very clearly argues not only for an eventual reduction in the debt, but also for its eventual retirement. His arguments echo classical republican virtue in decrying the accumulation of too much debt over time.

> There are respectable individuals, who from a just aversion to an accumulation of Public debt, are unwilling to concede to it any kind of utility. . . . Neither will it follow, that an accumulation of debt is desireable, because a certain degree of it operates as capital.[14]

Hamilton was not an advocate for government control of the economy, though. That much is clear from his statements. For him, the free competition between businesses would have many desirable outcomes, such as the elimination of monopolies, and the reduction in price of commodities to the lowest point possible. So, Hamilton argued government encouragement, but not control, of manufacturing would in the long run benefit the people at large. Even agriculture, often seen as antagonistic to manufacturing, would benefit, as lower prices for manufactured goods would result in increased personal wealth even for farmers. This is a consistent theme with Hamilton, that government exists for the benefit of the people.

Hamilton also echoed the sentiments of many of his contemporaries, as well as people today, in expressing concern for the United States' balance of trade with other countries. Showing a more mercantilist aspect to his thought, he emphasized that manufacturing would lead to a richer nation overall, and a better (i.e., positive) balance of trade with other countries. Agriculture alone cannot supply this benefit to the United States, though.

In stark contrast to an emphasis on a lack of wealth being necessary for republican virtue, as found in other writers, Hamilton stressed the need for wealth in order to achieve the best possible sort of political arrangements. In order for the supply of specie in the United States to increase, there would need to exist a more well-rounded economy than what was current. Manufacturing would lead to wealth, and wealth to strengthened independence and security from other nations.

He pointed to the United States' inability to supply itself during the Revolutionary War as illustrative of the problems the country would continue to face if it did not develop manufacturing as soon as possible. For Hamilton, the United States had been altogether too reliant on supplies and other forms of assistance from France in gaining its independence from Great Britain. Specifically, the United States needed a Navy, which unfortunately, following classical republican doctrine, had been completely disbanded after the end of the Revolution. In any case, it is historically true that French victories at sea enabled joint French/American victories on land such as Yorktown.

> Not only the wealth; but the independence and security of a Country, appear to be materially connected with the prosperity of manufactures.[15]

Why is this important for the United States? Why encourage manufacturing? Because doing so will help "establish *substantial* and *permanent order*." Again and again with Hamilton we see an overriding emphasis on, and concern with, the tenuous nature of the continued existence of the United States. This recommendation regarding manufacturing is only one means by which Hamilton is convinced the United States will succeed in the long run.

> It is a truth as important as it is agreeable, and one to which it is not easy to imagine exceptions, that every thing tending to establish *substantial* and *permanent order*, in the affairs of a Country, to increase the total mass of industry and opulence, is ultimately beneficial to every part of it.[16]

Now is a critical moment for Hamilton. The United States needs to act immediately if it is to survive. Doing so will also lead to an increase in foreign investment in the United States, which will lead to an increased supply of specie, and improvement in the wealth of all Americans. In an argument once again quite similar to one of Madison's, as we will see below, the government of the United States must act to create a domestic market, because other nations' governments already do this. The goal of this policy is again the well-being of the American people.

> Considering a monopoly of the domestic market to its own manufacturers as the reigning policy of manufacturing Nations, a similar policy on the part of the United States in every proper instance, is dictated, it might almost be said, by the principles of distributive justice.[17]

One way to achieve these goals is to impose tariffs on foreign goods, which need to be higher in the case of goods from some foreign competitor to domestic manufacturers. Another option is to pay bounties for certain goods, although this option is much more problematic for Hamilton than tariffs. They are beneficial only when an industry is very young and are frequently a source of jealousy. Still, there are benefits to the country as a whole from bounties, in his estimation. I myself am of the opinion that Hamilton shows here in his opinions on bounties that he himself was far more high-minded, and personally focused on the common good rather than his own self-interest, than other people were then, or now. He just never shows the malevolent calculation so many have characterized him as having. That bounties could be a source of corruption seems not to have even occurred to him.

It is with his argument in favor of the Constitutionality of his proposals that we come to the heart of the disagreement between Hamilton and Madison on the question of government involvement in the economy. There is an enormous divide between the two on this issue, and each individual's arguments on this point show a continuation of his preferences prior to the existence of the Constitution. For Hamilton, one cannot include all the details of what the federal government is permitted to do within the Constitution itself. This is once again indicative of his willingness to construe far, far more latitude into the Constitution regarding the powers of the federal government.

It is his appeal to the "general welfare" clause as the source for the Constitutionality of his proposals which so infuriated Madison, as we shall see below. Hamilton argues, in response to objections like Madison's, that this is not a power for the federal government to do whatever it wants. There is a limit, and it is that only actions may be taken that benefit the United States as a whole, and not any one part or state.

It is important to note, though, that Hamilton makes essentially the same argument as Madison, that "all" those who wrote the Constitution were in agreement, and had clear, unambiguous expectations as to how it would be interpreted and carried out, since as he says, it is "doubtless" that his interpretation is the correct one. This argument has been commented on frequently in Madison's case, but we see the same claim with Hamilton as well. I find the claim by both to be dubious at best. Neither can legitimately claim to have known the minds of all the other individuals who took part in writing the Constitution. Neither can lay claim to exclusive expertise in determining, once and for all, the meaning of its many passages which admit of more than one interpretation. I argue both had clear ideas of his own, but could not possibly be the one, final, source regarding the expectations all the other authors had.

> A Question has been made concerning the Constitutional right of the Government of the United States to apply this species of encouragement, but there is certainly no good foundation for such a question. . . . The terms "general Welfare" were doubtless intended to signify more than was expressed or imported in those which Preceded; otherwise numerous exigencies incident to the affairs of a Nation would have been left without a provision.[18]

In bemoaning the influence of state-centered opinions and loyalties, Hamilton as always displays his much more national focus for the United States.

> But if the legislature of the Union cannot do all the good, that might be wished, it is at least desirable, that all may be done, which is practicable.[19]

Hamilton had even more in mind for federal government involvement in the economy. Beyond encouraging manufacturing, he wanted for the federal government, taking a cue from a step already taken by individual states, to have a role in inspecting goods to ensure their quality. Far before the creation of the federal government agencies we take for granted today, Hamilton saw a need for consumer protection by the federal government. These inspections would, in his view, prevent fraud, improve quality, and more firmly establish the reputations of American goods.

Also, he argued for a much greater involvement by the federal government in financial exchanges, both to make such possible in the first place, and also to ease the process by which they would occur. Hamilton desired an expansion in the supply of money, especially paper money, and argued for the need for such paper to be good in every state. Internal improvements, especially, were an issue Hamilton regarded as needing national supervision. On their own, each state would focus solely on its own good, and their efforts would probably be not only wasteful due to repetition, but also counterproductive by coming into conflict with other states' efforts.

Hamilton showed he was in favor of, and willing to have, the Treasury take action to help stabilize the economy when needed. This is yet again indicative of Hamilton's much greater vision for the federal government's involvement in the economy than Madison's. In regard to a potential early bank panic, he wrote to William Seton in 1792 that he was willing to have the Treasury assist a prominent bank, in order to fend off the effects of what he considered unprincipled economic behavior by others.

> Be Confidential with me. If you are pressed, whatever support may be in my power shall be afforded. I consider the public interest as materially involved in aiding a valuable institution like yours to withstand the attacks of a confederated host of frantic and I fear, in too many instances, unprincipled gamblers.[20]

Hamilton even had in mind a role for the federal government as regards what we now call social programs, when and where those would be necessary. In a report sent to the Speaker of the House from 1792, he wrote:

> The establishment of one or more marine Hospitals in the United States is a measure desirable on various accounts.[21]

Notice the suggestion that a tax be levied, out of individual incomes, for the benefit of others. Now, the tax would be paid by those within a specific profession for the benefit of others in that profession, but this clearly shows that Hamilton thought of roles for the federal government that far exceeded the opinions of others of his time. Some people needed to be helped in order to be safe from want and misery, help that government could offer. Not only were the sailors to be protected, but also their wives and children. However, there were limits to what he felt government, and he in his official capacity as Treasury Secretary, could do.

> I regret much every embarassment which is experienced by the Mercantile Body—whether arising from the public operations, from accidental and unavoidable causes, or from a spirit of enterprise beyond the Capital which is to support it. . . .
>
> I do not perceive however that I can at the present moment contribute to this end otherwise than by encouraging the Bank to continue its aids as liberally as shall be consistent with its safety under an assurance that I shall for some time to come forbear drafts upon them as much as shall be practicable.[22]

Again, the goal for Hamilton behind all of his preferences for government involvement in the economy is the good of the people at large. Beyond helping to create better economic conditions, he argued government needed to be active to protect the people from various dangers, such as the "rich and powerful," and "caballers, intriguers, and demagogues." He also showed he was far more concerned about the possibility of anarchy than tyranny. Writing as "Tully" in 1794, he said,

> If it were to be asked, What is the most sacred duty and the greatest source of security in a Republic? the answer would be, An inviolable respect for the Constitution and Laws—the first growing out of the last. It is by this, in a great degree, that the rich and powerful are to be restrained from enterprises against the common liberty—operated upon by the influence of a general sentiment, by their interest in the principle, and by the obstacles which the habit it produces erects against innovation and encroachment.[23]

In the draft he wrote for George Washington's address, which I include here because the document at this point does reflect only Hamilton's ideas, and not Washington's, Hamilton argues it is "natural" to have a bureaucracy dedicated to taking care of not just manufacturing, but agriculture as well. Agriculture is so important that government "has" to oversee it to ensure the well-being of the country. Damage could potentially be done to agriculture due to a lack of oversight, and further, government action would, in Hamilton's estimation, result in greater strength, opulence, and happiness for the country as a whole.

I want to call attention to Hamilton's use of that word, "opulence." He uses it frequently in his writings, and it shows one of the ways in which Hamilton departed from a strictly classical understanding of the needs of a republic. In contrast to the classical emphasis on simplicity, even poverty, Hamilton argues for the need for greater wealth among the population as a whole in order for the United States to survive and thrive.

Hamilton also argues the need for the federal government to have a role in education, such as a national university and a national military academy. There are other schools, but he states they simply do not have enough money at this point to meet the needs of the nation. Also, the national university would attract students from all over the country, which would bring the United States closer together, as the students would receive a common education and experience that they would take back to their homes, and thus cause that national perspective to be more widely diffused throughout the country. The military academy would also provide a national point of view to those who serve in the military, rather than retaining a state-centered view, such as with state militia-only service.

He states his fear of a nation "subdivided," a notion which once again shows that he, in marked contrast to so many of his contemporaries, understood the United States to be one whole, and not a collection of states which just happen to have been gathered into one. As became clear over time, the view of the United States as a collection of states gathered together, or confederated, was one which persisted for decades, and was put to rest (for the most part) only by the Civil War.

Another point he raises, which proved to be quite controversial, is his call for a United States navy. After the end of the Revolutionary War, the United States had sold off its ships. However, if the United States wants to continue the commerce it has already established with other nations, it needs to protect it with a navy. The United States should remain neutral as regards the conflicts between other nations, of course, but nevertheless needs its own navy in order to induce other countries to actually respect that neutrality, as the United States was already learning in its attempt to stay out of the wars between Great Britain and France. This is yet another point on which he and Madison actually agreed more than they disagreed.

Further, in regard to pay for public servants, Hamilton argues that appeals to republican virtue are pointless. If the United States wants qualified individuals, it has to pay sufficiently well to attract and retain them. Not paying well limits public service to the rich. Hamilton again and again pointed out the limits of the republican virtue ideal. Humans do have selfish motives, which cannot be overcome by high-minded appeals alone. This is in fact quite similar to Madison's views of human nature in the *Federalist Papers*.

Hamilton, again in reference to the United States' relations with Great Britain, shows his far greater focus on building up the United States, rather than maintaining an intimate relationship with Great Britain, as Elkins and McKitrick depict him. He wanted to reduce the United States' dependence on Great Britain, something encouraging manufacturing would help, because depending on Great Britain would be a threat to American security. Specifically, as regards manufacturing, war-related industries need to be encouraged and built up to keep the United States safe. Publicly owned industries should be avoided but may be necessary if private industry cannot supply something absolutely necessary for defense.

> Nothing appears to [be] so unexceptionable & likely to be more efficacious than the institution of a Board of Agriculture with the views I have mentioned & with a moderate fund towards executing them. . . .
>
> I will however observe that if it be thought expedient the objects of the Board may be still more comprehensive. It may embrace the encouragement of the mechanic and manufacturing arts by means analogous to those for the improvement of Agriculture & with an eye to the introduction from abroad of useful machinery &c. Or there may be separate Boards one charged with one object the other with the other.
>
> I have heretofore suggested the expediency of establishing a national university and a Military Academy. . . .
>
> The Assembly to which I address myself will not doubt that the extension of science and knowledge is an object primarily interesting to our national welfare. . . . Or can it be doubted that this great object would be materially advanced by a University erected on that broad basis to which the national resources are most adequate & so liberally endowed as to command the ablest professors in the several branches of liberal knowlege? . . . Amongst the motives to such an institution the assimilation of the principles opinions manners and habits of our countrymen by drawing from all quarters our youth to participate in a common Education well deserves the attention of Government. To render the people of this Country as homogeneous as possible must lend as much as any other circumstance to the permanency of the Union & prosperity.
>
> The eligibleness of a Military Academy depends on that evident maxim of policy which requires every nation to be prepared for war while cultivating peace and warns it against suffering the military spirit & military knowlege wholly to decay. . . .
>
> A systematic plan for the creation of a moderate navy appears to me recommended by very weighty considerations. An active external Commerce demands a naval power to protect it—Besides the dangers from War in which a state is a party. . . .
>
> There is a subject which has dwelt long & much upon my mind which I cannot omit this opportunity of suggesting. It is the compensations to our public Officers; especially those in the most important stations. Every man acquainted [with] the expence even of the most frugal plan of living in our great cities must be sensible of their inadequateness. The impolicy of such defective provision seems not to have been sufficiently weighed.[24]

There are some limits on what government should do, according to Hamilton. There is such a thing as an "excess of regulation," but how to determine what is a good idea and what not? For Hamilton, one needs the appropriate kind of administrators, men of "sound judgement," and NOT what Hamilton referred to as "theorists," which as is well-known, was what he called Jefferson, Madison, and others who shared their opinions on government. Hamilton enunciates an Aristotelian argument in arguing for a "medium," and not "general principles," to determine how government should act. Once the Federalists had lost the election of 1800, and Democratic-Republican policies were put into place by the Jefferson Administration, Hamilton wrote in *The Examination* Number XI from 1802:

> It is certainly possible to do too much as well as too little; to embarrass, if not defeat the good which may be done, by attempting more than is practicable; or to overbalance that good by evils accruing from an excess of regulation. . . . To reach and not to pass the salutary medium is the province of sound judgment: To miss the point will ever be the lot of those who, enveloped all their lives in the mists of theory, are constantly seeking for an ideal perfection which never was and never will be attainable in reality. It is about this medium, not about general principles, that those in power in our government have differed; and to experience, not to the malevolent insinuations of rivals, must be the appeal, whether the one or the other description of persons have judged most accurately.[25]

NOTES

1. Harold C. Syrett, ed., and Jacob E. Cooke, assoc. ed., *The Papers of Alexander Hamilton*, volume III: 1782–1786 (New York: Columbia University Press, 1962), 75–76.
2. Ibid, 78.
3. Ibid, 82.
4. Ibid, 99.
5. Ibid, 100.
6. Ibid, 100–103.
7. Ibid, 104.
8. Ibid, 105–106.
9. Harold C. Syrett, ed., and Jacob E. Cooke, assoc. ed., *The Papers of Alexander Hamilton*, volume VIII: February 1791–July 1792 (New York: Columbia University Press, 1965), 300–301.
10. Harold C. Syrett, ed., and Jacob E. Cooke, assoc. ed., *The Papers of Alexander Hamilton*, volume IX: August 1791–December 1791 (New York: Columbia University Press, 1965), 144–145.
11. Ibid, 249.
12. Ibid, 262–263.
13. Ibid, 277.
14. Ibid, 282–283.
15. Ibid, 290–291.
16. Ibid, 294.
17. Ibid, 297.
18. Ibid, 302–304.
19. Ibid, 308.

20. Ibid, 562–563.

21. Harold C. Syrett, ed., and Jacob E. Cooke, assoc. ed., *The Papers of Alexander Hamilton*, volume XI: February 1792–June 1792 (New York: Columbia University Press, 1966), 295.

22. Harold C. Syrett, ed., and Jacob E. Cook, assoc. ed., *The Papers of Alexander Hamilton*, volume XIV: February 1793–June 1793 (New York: Columbia University Press, 1969), 283–284.

23. Harold C. Syrett, ed., and Jacob E. Cook, assoc. ed., *The Papers of Alexander Hamilton*, volume XVII: August 1794–December 1794 (New York: Columbia University Press, 1972), 159.

24. Harold C. Syrett, ed., *The Papers of Alexander Hamilton*, volume XX: January 1796–March 1797 (New York: Columbia University Press, 1974), 382–388.

25. Harold C. Syrett, ed., *The Papers of Alexander Hamilton*, volume XXV: July 1800–April 1802 (New York: Columbia University Press, 1977), 514–515.

Chapter Seven

Madison on the Federal Government's Role in the Economy

Madison also valued a role for the federal government in the economy, but not in the same ways, and not to the same degree, as Hamilton. One area in which he saw a drastically different role for the federal government in the economy was to use economic relations with other countries as a weapon, especially through the use of embargoes against countries he felt the United States had legitimate grievances with. The role Madison saw as a valuable addition to the eventual success of the United States was, as I will show below, in encouraging agriculture, *not* manufacturing, as Hamilton wanted.

With James Madison what we really see is a difference of opinion with Hamilton in degree. In so many ways, their conflicts reflected not a vast gulf of different principles, but rather different priorities. There were some issues on which they differed markedly, but these are the exception. Sadly, each interpreted the other's actions in the worst manner possible. Fear, rather than giving the benefit of the doubt, ruled both. Like Hamilton, Madison also saw the need for the federal government to have the power to regulate trade during the time of the Articles of Confederation. For Madison, the states simply cannot effectively regulate trade by themselves. There needed to be a common overseer of trade for the United States, just like other countries had.

Again, like Hamilton, Madison argued that free trade with other countries would be the ideal, but it was just not possible at that time, due to the policies of other governments. Given that reality, the United States needed to enact similar policies to protect itself. A tariff would be the best option for not only controlling trade, giving the United States leverage in negotiations with other countries, and equally important, paying off the debt owed to other countries. To James Monroe he wrote in 1785:

> Viewing in the abstract the question whether the power of regulating trade, to a certain degree at least, ought to be vested in Congress, it appears to me not to admit of a doubt, but that it should be decided in the affirmative. . . . A perfect freedom is the System which would be my choice. But before such a system will be eligible perhaps for the U. S. they must be out of debt; before it will be attainable, all other nations must concur in it.[1]

With Madison more so than Hamilton, though, we see the notion of using trade with other countries as a weapon. Other than in the *Federalist Papers*, Hamilton does not mention this as an option for the federal government. With Madison, especially in his nonofficial papers, this idea occurs far more often. The United States must be able to, for instance, "extort redress" from other countries. Again, to Monroe in the same letter as above he wrote:

> Must we remain passive victims to foreign politics; or shall we exert the lawful means which our independence has put into our hands, of extorting redress? The very question would be an affront to every Citizen who loves his Country. . . . How is this harmony to be obtained? only by an acquiescence of all the States in the opinion of a reasonable majority.[2]

At first, Madison wanted amendments to be made to the Articles of Confederation. He did not initially want a quite different form of government, which the Constitution eventually was. However, the "machinations" of Great Britain needed to be dealt with, and only a stronger federal government could do that.

> But let us not sacrifice the end to the means: let us not rush on certain ruin in order to avoid a possible danger. I conceive it to be of great importance that the defects of the fœderal system should be amended, not only because such amendments will make it better answer the purpose for which it was instituted, but because I apprehend danger to its very existence from a continuance of defects which expose a part if not the whole of the empire to severe distress.[3]

Not just Great Britain needs to be dealt with, but also some American citizens are behaving in ways contrary to the nation's best interest. Specifically, Madison identifies the "mercantile interest" as being far too closely aligned with Great Britain than the United States. We saw this above with Hamilton's concern with the "trading interest." Madison identifies the continued animosity toward Great Britain as a resource which could be made use of in order to counteract the baleful influence of the merchants and Great Britain.

> Add to all this that the mercantile interest which has taken the lead in rousing the public attention of other States, is in this so exclusively occupied in British

Commerce that what little weight they have will be most likely to fall into the opposite scale.[4]

The malignant influence of Great Britain is something that was clearly much more on Madison's mind than Hamilton's, although Hamilton did decry a lack of American ability to deal on more equal terms with other countries. He was just far more concerned about *both* France and Great Britain than Madison was. In any case, we see again and again in Madison's writings a focus on dealing specifically with Great Britain, and he hoped that the people at large would become fed up with the ways in which Great Britain was treating the United States, thus agreeing to give the federal government more power. His home state of Virginia was especially recalcitrant in Madison's estimation, mainly due to the recovery in the prices it was receiving for its farm exports. Madison was especially afraid that Great Britain's ultimate goal was to affect a disunion of the United States. To Thomas Jefferson he wrote in 1785:

> A *majority* of *the states* deprived of a *regular remidy for their distresses* by *the want* of *a fœderal spirit in the minority* must *feel the* strongest *motives to some ir*regular *experiments*. The *dan*[ger] *of such a crisis* makes me surmise that the *policy of Great Britain* results as much from *the hope of effecting a breach in our confederacy* as *of monopolising our trade*.[5]

To George Washington in 1785 he expressed his conclusion that the reason behind the states' refusal to grant the federal government more control over commerce came down to simple fear. Madison showed his classical education by comparing the situation the United States was in to that of the Greek city-states just prior to their conquest by Macedonia. Like the Greek confederation, Madison thought the United States was in danger because it had not granted its general government enough power to effectively deal with foreign countries.

> Those whose opposition in this case did not spring from illiberal animosities towards the Northern States, seem to have been frightened on one side at the idea of a perpetual & irrevocable grant of power, and on the other flattered with a hope, that a temporary grant might be renewed from time to time, if its utility should be confirmed by the experiment. But we have already granted perpetual & irrevocable powers of a much more extensive nature than those now proposed and for reasons not stronger than the reasons which urge the latter. And as to the hope of renewal, it is the most visionary one that perhaps ever deluded men of sense. Nothing but the peculiarity of our circumstances could ever have produced those sacrifices of sovereignty on which the fœderal Government now rests.[6]

In contrast to Hamilton, where most of our sources of his ideas come from his writings, with Madison we fortunately also have a wealth of his thoughts given through his speeches in the Continental Congress, the legislature of Virginia, and also the Congress of the United States. As regards the question of direct taxation by the federal government, even during his service in the Continental Congress, Madison stressed the need for the federal government to have the power of directly taxing the people, rather than that of sending requisitions to the states, in order to have better control of the United States' economy. Specifically, the federal government needed to be able to pay the country's debts, most especially those owed overseas, but could only do so if it had the ability to levy taxes without state interference.

> My honorable friend seems to think that we ought to spare the present generation, and throw our burthens upon posterity. I will not contest the equity of this reasoning, but I must say that good policy as well as views of œconomy, strongly urge us even to distress ourselves to comply with our most solemn engagements. We must make effectual provision for the payment of the interest of our public debts. In order to do justice to our creditors, and support our credit and reputation; we must lodge power some where or other for this purpose.[7]

While not stressing the issue as much as Hamilton, Madison also expressed a greater fear of state power than federal power. This once again shows the differences between the two were quite often ones of degree than of differing principles. From the same speech in the Continental Congress as above, Madison expressed his conviction that the federal government needed to have the ability to "suppress" state power if necessary.

> I do not thoroughly comprehend the reasoning of my honorable friend, when he tells us, that the federal government will predominate, and that the state interest will be lost; when at the same time he tells us, that it will be a faction of seven states. If seven states will prevail *as states*, I conceive that state influence will prevail. If state influence under the present feeble government has prevailed, I think that a remedy ought to be introduced by giving the general government power to suppress it.[8]

Both Madison and Hamilton wanted the United States to remain neutral in the ongoing European conflicts, most notably those between France and Great Britain. Both argued in favor of the United States building and maintaining a navy in order to enforce its neutrality, as both Great Britain and France had interfered with American shipping because the United States simply did not have a naval force with which to protect itself. Madison, in stark contrast to Hamilton, though, did not like having to have a standing military establishment. He nevertheless saw the need for one, given the realities of how other countries treated the United States.

> He supposed that my argument with respect to a future war between Great-Britain and France was fallacious. The other nations of Europe have acceded to that neutrality while Great-Britain opposed it. We need not expect in case of such a war, that we should be suffered to participate of the profitable emoluments of the carrying trade, unless we were in a respectable situation. Recollect the last war. Was there ever a war in which the British nation stood opposed to so many nations? All the belligerent nations in Europe, with nearly one half of the British empire, were united against it. Yet that nation, though defeated, and humbled beyond any previous example, stood out against this. From her firmness and spirit in such desperate circumstances, we may divine what her future conduct may be. I did not contend that it was necessary for the United States to establish a navy for that sole purpose, but instanced it as one reason out of several, for rendering ourselves respectable. I am no friend to naval or land armaments in time of peace, but if they be necessary, the calamity must be submitted to. Weakness will invite insults. A respectable government will not only intitle us to a participation of the advantages which are enjoyed by other nations, but will be a security against attacks and insults. It is to avoid the calamity of being obliged to have large armaments that we should establish this government. The best way to avoid danger, is to be in a capacity to withstand it.[9]

Madison's efforts in regard to creating a stronger union through government involvement in the economy did not stop when he helped achieve his goal of ratifying the Constitution. As he began his service in the House of Representatives, Madison again stressed the imperative that the United States put its finances in order. Madison still wanted as much free trade as possible but given the continued reality of tariff usage by other countries, he again argued in favor of not only the necessity, but the utility as well, of the United States making use of tariffs.

> The deficiency in our treasury has been too notorious to make it necessary for me to animadvert upon that subject.[10]

Madison, in contrast to Hamilton, argued for the need to focus more on current revenue concerns than promoting manufactures. Here is in fact a very important point to understand in regard to the differences the two had, and the effects those differences had on the United States. Manufacturing was simply not as important for Madison as it was for Hamilton. He did assume manufacturing would eventually be added to a more diversified American economy, but in so many ways he dreaded that eventuality, given his conviction that a more manufacturing-based economy would be a threat to the republican virtue on which the United States ultimately depended.

> It was my view to restrain the first essay on this subject principally to the object of revenue, and make this rather a temporary expedient than any thing permanent.[11]

Madison did consistently display his more nationalistic preferences by urging others in the nascent Congress of the United States to focus on the common needs of the country as a whole, rather than just the needs of their individual states.

> But on the other hand, we must limit our consideration on this head, and notwithstanding all the deference and respect we pay to those sentiments, we must consider the general interest of the union,[12]

While nowhere near as convinced of their importance as Hamilton, Madison did not completely oppose the encouragement of manufacturing by the federal government, now that such power had been granted to Congress by the Constitution. Nevertheless, he once again expressed his preference for a free market, rather than extensive government control of the economy.

> In the first place, I own myself the friend to a very free system of commerce, and hold it as a truth, that commercial shackles are generally unjust, oppressive and impolitic—it is also a truth, that if industry and labour are left to take their own course, they will generally be directed to those objects which are the most productive, and this in a more certain and direct manner than the wisdom of the most enlightened legislature could point out.[13]

Madison also thought the federal government should take similar steps to encourage agriculture, in which he argued the United States already had advantages over other countries, in order to counterbalance the advantages European countries had in manufacturing.

> In my opinion, it would be proper also, for gentlemen to consider the means of encouraging the great staple of America, I mean agriculture, which I think may justly be stiled the staple of the United States.[14]

In addition to actions he believed the federal government needed to take to involve itself in the economy due to the policies of other governments, Madison argued there were other exceptions to an overall policy of free trade that would be necessary. Tariffs are one, but also where tariffs have been used to help create businesses, the federal government needs to continue to protect them, since they are dependent upon government aid. In keeping with his republican virtue focus, Madison also sees a role for sumptuary laws, in order to encourage appropriate civic virtue amongst the citizens. Embargoes during war are another case, as well as protections for defense-related industries.

But, in contrast to Hamilton, Madison argued these sorts of protections are not as important as many think. The experiences the United States had during the Revolutionary War are not as clear a lesson for Madison as for Hamilton. Mainly, he was not as convinced of the need for federally protected defense-related industries if they were too expensive. He argued that, even in war, the United States would be able to obtain supplies from abroad. Finally, Madison introduces an income-based argument in favor of tariffs, as being a just way to tax the rich instead of the poor, since the amount of tax paid would be in proportion to the differing levels of consumption by those two groups.

> The difficulties we experienced a few years ago, of obtaining military supplies, ought not to furnish too much in favour of an establishment which would be difficult and expensive.[15]

Again, though, Madison did argue there were exceptions to his preference for free trade, but how to identify them would be left up to an examination of whether or not they were necessary for the common good. Specifically, any tariff, being a tax, should be apportioned to the ability of those affected by it to actually pay. He identified different effects of tariffs on variously the poor and the rich and decried what he considered unjust amounts expected out of either.

> I readily agree, that in itself a tax would be unjust and oppressive that did not fall on the citizens according to their degree of property and ability to pay it.[16]

It was the differences among the states as regards economic regulation that led Madison to consider it necessary for the federal government to step in. In some cases, the states did not have any regulations at all on various points, such as tariff collection, while others specifically prohibited any state official from enforcing federal regulations. So, it became necessary in Madison's opinion for the federal government to establish its own means, and the officials to carry them out, in order for any tariff to be collected. Thus, it is in this case precisely the states' refusal to take action that caused the federal government to establish a bureaucracy it might not have had to otherwise, had it been able to rely on state officials to collect the tariff.

However, Madison clearly mentions below a major point of disagreement with Hamilton—that of encouraging manufacturing by the federal government. Far from there being a pressing need for such action, Madison specifically identified any such decision as "premature." In a letter to Edmund Pendleton in 1789 he wrote:

> If the duties should be raised too high, the error will proceed as much from the popular ardor to throw the burden of revenue on trade, as from the premature policy of stimulating manufactures.[17]

Elkins and McKitrick, in their *The Age of Federalism*, have, as I have discussed earlier in this work, characterized the main difference between Hamilton and Madison as following from the different preferences each had as regards France and Great Britain, the two "superpowers" of the day. I have taken issue with that, but there is some evidence that, at least in Madison's case, he did indeed have a preference for France, but only up until the time Napoleon took over. This preference for France was at first based on gratitude for help during the Revolution, but then after the French Revolution it was based on support for a kindred republican state. The effect of this support did, while it lasted, give him a reason to support federal government involvement in the economy in favor of relations with France. For Madison, this was in part supported by his conviction that the public at large wanted France to have privileges other countries did not.

> Some gentlemen have seemed to call in question the policy of discriminating between nations in commercial alliance with the United States, and those with whom no treaties exist; for my own part, I am well satisfied that there are good and substantial reasons for making it; in the first place, it may not be unworthy of consideration, that the public sentiments of America will be favourable to such discrimination.[18]

Sometimes for Madison, the need for federal government involvement in the economy comes from, as in the case with Great Britain, where the free market has not resulted in the optimal situation, due to previous political influences. In the case of these "unnatural" situations, it is appropriate for the federal government to correct the situation by various means. These "political advantages" given to some but not other countries will, in Madison's estimation, lead to greater economic exchange in those instances, correcting what he argues was a disproportionate amount of influence by Great Britain. Also, it would lead to other nations being more willing to make favorable trade agreements with the United States, in order to increase the amount of business with the United States.

> From artificial or adventitious causes the commerce between America and Great Britain exceeds what may be considered its natural boundary.[19]

The United States simply cannot have an overall blanket policy of free trade, at least at this point in its history, according to Madison. The other countries of the world just do not follow that line of reasoning, and so the

United States must behave in a similar manner. When it is in the United States' interest, it can follow a free market approach, but when it is not, it must nevertheless follow its interest, and not the principle of free trade.

> I wish we were under less necessity than I find we are to shackle our commerce with duties, restrictions and preferences; but there are cases in which it is impossible to avoid following the example of other nations in the great diversity of our trade.[20]

In some ways, though, Madison wanted to have the federal government direct commerce just as much as Hamilton, but in a different direction. He argued for the need to have the federal government counteract powerful interests and individuals in society. Especially, the federal government needed to behave in ways to overcome established wealth, which would lead to greater equality amongst citizens.

> I cannot help conceiving that, from the force of habit and other conspiring causes, that nation is in possession of a much greater proportion of our trade than she naturally is intitled to.[21]

In an argument similar to one of Hamilton's in favor of encouraging manufactures, Madison argues the federal government needs to counteract old habits leading to more trade with some countries than with others. Madison did agree with Hamilton on the need for a navy, given the United States' interest in foreign commerce via its own ships. Otherwise, the United States would have to rely on the ships of other countries and would lose out on much of the wealth flowing from that business. Also, he argued it would be a good thing for the United States to have its own commercial ships, because they would supply the sailors it would need for a navy in case of a war. Overall, giving preferences to some but not other countries, combined with merchant shipping, would lead in Madison's opinion, to greater safety for the United States.

Madison ties the importance of republican virtue to the idea of a free market, which is actually a departure in many ways from earlier writers on the subject. For Madison, though, a free market is in his view essential for the success of the United States' experiment in republican government. However, the farming lifestyle is the best, indeed essential, way of making a living to help create the republican virtues needed. Manufacturing can only be done in cities, which are anathema to the independence and self-reliance necessary for a republican lifestyle. Writing for the *National Gazette* in 1792, he said,

> A PERFECT theory on this subject would be useful, not because it could be reduced to practice by any plan of legislation, or ought to be attempted by violence on the will or property of individuals: but because it would be a monition

against empirical experiments by power, and a model to which the free choice of occupations by the people, might gradually approximate the order of society.

The best distribution is that which would most favor *health, virtue, intelligence* and *competency* in the *greatest number* of citizens. It is needless to add to these objects, *liberty* and *safety*. The first is presupposed by them. The last must result from them.

The life of the husbandman is pre-eminently suited to the comfort and happiness of the individual. *Health*, the first of blessings, is an appurtenance of his property and his employment. *Virtue*, the health of the soul, is another part of his patrimony, and no less favored by his situation. *Intelligence* may be cultivated in this as well as in any other walk of life. If the mind be less susceptible of polish in retirement than in a croud, it is more capable of profound and comprehensive efforts. Is it more ignorant of some things? It has a compensation in its ignorance of others. *Competency* is more universally the lot of those who dwell in the country, when liberty is at the same time their lot. The extremes both of want and of waste have other abodes. 'Tis not the country that peoples either the Bridewells or the Bedlams. These mansions of wretchedness are tenanted from the distresses and vices of overgrown cities.[22]

Again and again, Madison emphasized that agriculture, rather than manufacturing, was the path to the independence, happiness and public liberty for everyone that classical republican virtue offered. To help achieve this goal, he did approve of government involvement in the economy. For Madison, there was no need to promote manufacturing, with its baleful effects on virtue, but government could employ itself profitably by promoting farming.

The class of citizens who provide at once their own food and their own raiment, may be viewed as the most truly independent and happy. They are more: they are the best basis of public liberty, and the strongest bulwark of public safety. It follows, that the greater the proportion of this class to the whole society, the more free, the more independent, and the more happy must be the society itself.

In appreciating the regular branches of manufacturing and mechanical industry, their tendency must be compared with the principles laid down, and their merits graduated accordingly. Whatever is least favorable to vigor of body, to the faculties of the mind, or to the virtues or the utilities of life, instead of being forced or fostered by public authority, ought to be seen with regret as long as occupations more friendly to human happiness, lie vacant.

The several professions of more elevated pretensions, the merchant, the lawyer, the physician, the philosopher, the divine, form a certain proportion of every civilized society, and readily adjust their numbers to its demands, and its circumstances.[23]

Madison was not always entirely consistent on this point, though. He did sometimes support government actions taken on behalf of manufacturing. If it came down to the continued existence of an already established industry, he was willing to make exceptions.

> Mr. Madison thought it was worthy of consideration, whether it would not be expedient to make an exception in favour of white cotton goods. He understood there was a manufactory of some consequence established in this country, whose business it was to print these white cottons, and if this exception was not made, this additional duty might go to the destruction of it. Indeed as the printing of this article added as he was informed, two-thirds to its value, it might be considered as a raw material. He believed this manufactory was carried on by persons who came from foreign countries. If their manufactory succeeded, it might induce others to follow them, to exercise their several professions amongst us, which could not fail to be of advantage to the country; but if the present manufactory should be destroyed by one of our laws bearing hard upon its proprietors, it would have quite a contrary effect. He owned he was not much acquainted with the manufactory in question, nor had he made much calculation upon the subject; but, from the face of it, it seemed to require an exception. He therefore made the motion.[24]

Even though, as I have shown above, Hamilton and Madison did have underlying differences in their expectations for the United States, specifically in this case on what, if any, role the federal government would have in the economy, in more ways they were actually quite similar rather than having dramatic differences of opinion. That they did not give each other the benefit of the doubt, and immediately attributed the different preferences each had to some kind of betrayal of the American Revolution, is indicative of not only how humans have perceived each other historically, but on an ongoing basis. Rather than just understanding that intelligent people of good will can and do quite often come to different conclusions regarding the questions of the day, Hamilton and Madison made the same mistake people continue to make today, seeing only what they fear in the actions of others, rather than recognizing that actions can, and do, reflect a wide range of motivations.

Between the two, Madison is more hesitant than Hamilton to have the federal government involve itself extensively in the economy, but this is a difference in degree, and not principle. Both wanted the new federal government to correct the problems that had occurred under the Articles of Confederation. Just how to do so, and what underlying Constitutional support for any actions taken, were the areas on which they differed.

Both agreed on the need for tariffs, but Madison was, as we have seen, much more interested in using these to achieve not only the goal of revenue for the federal government, but also as a tool for use in foreign relations. He clearly wanted to shift the United States' economy away from primary trade with Great Britain toward a much more diversified situation, especially by giving France greater benefits. Hamilton seemed much more content with the trade situation with Great Britain, but clearly wanted the United States to become more independent over time through expanding its own manufacturing base.

The goal both had at all times, though, does show them to have been in essential ways far more similar than different. Each was concerned with, and proposed policies based on, the good of the American people as a whole. That they were unable to see this in each other, and give each other the benefit of the doubt, is an all too common tragic reality in American life which continues still to this day.

Republicanism for both Hamilton and Madison mandated government focus on the common good. However, they had different ideas about whether, to what extent, and what kinds of federal government activity were necessary to help the American republican experiment succeed. For Hamilton, that focus on the common good required the federal government take a widespread active role in the economy in order to provide a good standard of living for the American people. That way, the people would accept, and continue to support, the American republic. Further, this necessary, and good, federal government involvement in the economy required taxation. It would be through taxes that the United States could be effectively protected from threats at home and abroad, plus it would achieve respectability with other countries. For Hamilton, these need to be addressed for any kind of country, including a republic, to succeed.

Very different from Madison, Hamilton again and again included "Greatness" as one of his goals for the United States. Indeed, he listed greatness as one of the absolute vital necessities in order for the American republican experiment to succeed. Only in a large, wealthy, great republic could America survive and thrive. This is of course a departure from classical republican theory on Hamilton's part, but as we have seen, both departed from classical theory at various times.

With Madison, we see such a departure in his emphasis on a free market, with as little government regulation as possible, as necessary for the American republican experiment to succeed. Also, Madison did see a good, indeed vital, role for the federal government in the economy, but to encourage agriculture, not manufacturing as Hamilton wanted. The agricultural life was, far more for Madison than Hamilton, the best way to encourage the kind of civic virtue among citizens which would help the American republic succeed.

Interestingly, both Hamilton and Madison saw an important role for the federal government in the economy in order to counteract powerful economic interests within the United States itself with goals contrary to the common good. Hamilton identified the "trading interest," while Madison spoke of the "mercantile interest" as not having interests always in accordance with the good of the United States as a whole. That both agreed on the value of federal government involvement in the economy on this subject shows that their differences were not absolute, and it is simply too bad they could not see they had points on which they were in agreement.

NOTES

1. Robert A. Rutland, et.al, eds., *The Papers of James Madison*, Volume 8: 10 March 1784–28 March 1786 (Chicago: The University of Chicago Press, 1973), 333–334.
2. Ibid, 334.
3. Ibid, 334–335.
4. Ibid, 336.
5. Ibid, 344.
6. Ibid, 438–439.
7. Robert A. Rutland, et.al, eds., *The Papers of James Madison*, Volume 11: 7 March 1788–1 March 1789 (Chicago: The University of Chicago Press, 1977), 124.
8. Ibid, 124–125.
9. Ibid, 125.
10. Charles F. Hobson, et.al, eds., *The Papers of James Madison*, Volume 12: 2 March 1789–20 January 1790, with a supplement 24 October 1775–24 January 1789 (Chicago: The University of Chicago Press, 1979), 65.
11. Ibid, 69.
12. Ibid, 70.
13. Ibid, 70–71.
14. Ibid, 71–72.
15. Ibid, 72–73.
16. Ibid, 85–86.
17. Ibid, 89.
18. Ibid, 97–98.
19. Ibid, 98.
20. Ibid, 99.
21. Ibid, 100.
22. Robert A. Rutland, et.al, eds., *The Papers of James Madison*, Volume 14: 6 April 1791–16 March 1793 (Chicago: The University of Chicago Press, 1983), 244–245.
23. Ibid, 246.
24. J. C. A. Stagg, et.al, eds., *The Papers of James Madison*, Volume 16: 27 April 1795–27 March 1797 (Chicago: The University of Chicago Press, 1989), 496–497.

Conclusion

> "The oldest and strongest emotion of mankind is fear, and the oldest and strongest kind of fear is fear of the unknown."—H.P. Lovecraft[1]

As I conclude this book, I will focus on the overall implications for republicanism of the differing points of view Hamilton and Madison had. As I mentioned above, there is no one universal definition of the word "republic," and so what it means for the United States to be a republic has been a source of constant debate throughout its history. The differences Hamilton and Madison had will help highlight that debate, as both were pivotal figures in the early history of the United States, and their influence has continued to this day. This book has expanded the comparison of Hamilton and Madison into new areas that have not been as fully explored before. As I stated previously, this is my original contribution to the literature on Hamilton, Madison, Constitutional interpretation, and the early history of the U.S. republic.

Overall, the conflict between Hamilton and Madison is just one example of the difficulty in even defining the word "republic" precisely. I mentioned John Adams's letter to Mercy Warren in my Introduction, and how many different types of governments have been described as republics over history, and so it is not really possible to clearly identify any one kind of government as "the" one and only way to think of what a republic should be like. The problem Adams identified has not changed in the years since, so what can we take away from the material I have presented here?

First, it is important to understand that both Hamilton and Madison considered themselves republicans, and both were unalterably committed to the success of the United States as one, unified nation. Clearly, though, they had different ideas of what the United States would be like. I included the quote from H. P. Lovecraft at the beginning of this Conclusion, though, to begin to present my main contention as to what I think is the single most important implication for republicanism to take away from Hamilton and Madison's disagreements.

Both Hamilton and Madison considered their expectations for the United States as "the" one, correct and best vision for the United States. That they could not give each other the benefit of the doubt when their differences became apparent is, I argue, the result of the "fear of the unknown" Lovecraft cited. The United States was a very young country, which no one knew for sure whether or not it was going to succeed, and neither could accept the reality of anyone having a conflicting point of view of their own. Still to this day there is the completely unreasonable expectation among people of many different ideologies that theirs is the only possible way for the United States to survive and thrive. In that regard, sadly, nothing has changed since Hamilton and Madison.

The simple reality is, there have demonstrably been a wide variety of different visions for the United States over time, and with the single exception of the issue of slavery, the United States has managed to survive, and thrive enormously, for over two centuries. This desire for unanimity is simply unreasonable, counter-productive, and unattainable. There are many different ways of thinking about what a republic should be, and many different ways a country can find to survive and thrive. The United States has not finished, if that is even possible, defining the meaning of a republic, at least in its own case. The political process, which again has worked in almost all eras of the history of the United States, is the only peaceful alternative, so why not simply continue to make use of that in order to "define the republic?"

Far too many look to the Founders for a coherent vision for the United States. If nothing else, this book will, I hope, help to dispel that misconception. So many want the Founders to have had a coherent understanding of, and vision for, the United States, as a group. They simply did not. However, the influence of the Founders is vast, though not in regards to their agreements. Rather, it is their disagreements that have proven to be of lasting influence, which for instance initially resulted in the first two political parties in the United States, the Federalists and the Democratic-Republicans. The notion of having different political parties, to express and represent different underlying expectations for the United States, has not gone away, and why should it?

I entitled this book *Defining the Republic: Early Conflicts over the Constitution* initially because Hamilton and Madison had, in his own way, a definition. Their definitions differed, though, as I have shown. Such disagreements are inevitable. Humans are simply not capable of unanimity. In order for any country to succeed, it must find ways to resolve those differences of opinion, at least for a period of time, in a peaceful manner. While not perfect, if indeed any such standard of perfection is possible, the political process is far preferable to violence and bloodshed. It is to the political process that I argue the United States needs to look to "define the republic," at least for any one moment in time.

Hamilton and Madison's fear of each other, though, is an example of the major impediment to meaningful resolution, for any period of time, of disagreements over what the republic of the United States should be like. If people cannot recognize that disagreements do NOT mean the other person, or group, is going to destroy the country through the potential enactment of their policy preferences, conflicts like the Civil War are the only option left to provide a resolution. Fear simply cannot be allowed to govern the nation's political choices in all but a few circumstances.

That this sort of thing continues to be a problem has been remarked upon by Morris Fiorina in *Culture War?*

> Americans contrast the environments in which they live their lives with a political order dominated by activists and elected officials who behave like squabbling children in a crowded sandbox. This is another reason why Americans dislike politics: they are put off by the people who specialize in politics.
>
> In sum, there is a disconnect between the world of contemporary Americans and the political order that purports to represent them. Citizens see a political order that characteristically debates policy proposals more extreme than necessary to address societal issues and community problems, a political order that spends inordinate amounts of time debating policy issues that most citizens do not view as among the more important issues facing the country, and a political order dominated by a political class whose behavior and operating style would be unacceptable outside of politics.[2]

While Fiorina's argument seems to imply that sharp, perhaps even irreconcilable, differences between the different groups who comprise the political class is a development that is wholly recent, I argue that such differences have existed all along. Did most Americans care anywhere near as much about the creation of a national bank as did Hamilton and Madison? I hardly think so. Did most Americans really want a Civil War? Again, I hardly think so. Differences of viewpoint, leading to sometimes extreme conflicts, have been a characteristic of those who have come to lead here in America from the very beginning.

NOTES

1. H. P. Lovecraft, *Supernatural Horror in Literature*, 2nd edition, edited by S.T. Joshi (New York: Hippocampus Press, 2012), 25.
2. Morris P. Fiorina, with Samuel J. Abrams and Jeremy C. Pope, *Culture War? The Myth of a Polarized America*, Third Edition (Boston: Longman, 2011), 204–205.

Bibliography

Adair, Douglass and Martin Harvey, "Was Alexander Hamilton a Christian Statesman?" *The William and Mary Quarterly*, Third Series 12, No. 2 (1955), 308–329.

Adams, John and Mercy Warren, *Correspondence Between John Adams and Mercy Warren* (New York: Arno Press, 1972).

Banning, Lance, *The Sacred Fire of Liberty: James Madison and the Founding of the Federal Republic* (Ithaca: Cornell University Press, 1995).

Brugger, Robert J., et.al, eds. *The Papers of James Madison, Secretary of State Series*, Volume 1: 4 March–31 July 1801 (Charlottesville: University Press of Virginia, 1986).

Chernow, Ron, *Alexander Hamilton* (New York: The Penguin Press, 2004).

Cicero, *On the Commonwealth*, trans. by George Holland Sabine and Stanley Barney Smith (New York: MacMillan Publishing Company, 1976).

Elkins, Stanley and Eric McKitrick, *The Age of Federalism* (New York: Oxford University Press, 1993).

Fatovic, Clement, "Reason and Experience in Alexander Hamilton's Science of Politics," *American Political Thought* 2, No.1 (2013): 1–30.

Fiorina, Morris P., Samuel J. Abrams and Jeremy C. Pope, *Culture War? The Myth of a Polarized America* (Boston: Longman 2011).

Hackett, Mary A., et.al., eds. *The Papers of James Madison, Secretary of State Series*, Volume 2: 1 August 1801–28 February 1802 (Charlottesville: University Press of Virginia, 1993).

Harrington, James, *The Commonwealth of Oceana and A System of Politics*, ed. by J.G.A. Pocock (Cambridge: Cambridge University Press, 1992).

Hobbes, Thomas, *Leviathan*, ed. by Richard Tuck (Cambridge: Cambridge University Press, 1991).

Hobson, Charles F., et.al, eds., *The Papers of James Madison*, Volume 12: 2 March 1789–20 January 1790, with a supplement 24 October 1775–24 January 1789 (Chicago: The University of Chicago Press, 1979).

Hobson, Charles F., et.al, eds., *The Papers of James Madison*, Volume 13: 20 January 1790–31 March 1791 (Chicago: The University of Chicago Press, 1981).

Hume, David, "Idea of a Perfect Commonwealth," in *Essays, Moral, Political, and Literary*, ed. by Eugene F. Miller (Indianapolis: Liberty Fund, 1987).

Hutchinson, William T., and William M.E. Rachal, eds., *The Papers of James Madison*, Volume 1: 16 March 1751–16 December 1779 (Chicago: The University of Chicago Press, 1962).

Hutchinson, William T., and William M.E. Rachal, eds., *The Papers of James Madison*, Volume 2: 20 March 1780–23 February 1781 (Chicago: The University of Chicago Press, 1962).

Hutchinson, William T., and William M.E. Rachal, eds., *The Papers of James Madison*, Volume 6: 9 April 1786–24 May 1787 (Chicago: The University of Chicago Press, 1975).

Lindsay, Thomas, "James Madison on Religion and Politics: Rhetoric and Reality," *The American Political Science Review* 85, No. 4 (1991), 1321–1337.

Locke, John, *The Two Treatises of Government*, ed. by Peter Laslett (Cambridge: Cambridge University Press, 1988).

Lovecraft, H.P. "Supernatural Horror in Literature," http://www.hplovecraft.com/writings/texts/essays/shil.aspx, accessed November 1, 2015.

Lutz, Donald, "The Relative Influence of European Writers on Late Eighteenth Century American Political Thought." *The American Political Science Review* 78, no. 1 (1984): 189–197.

Mason, Thomas A., et.al, eds., *The Papers of James Madison*, Volume 15: 24 March 1793–20 April 1795 (Chicago: The University of Chicago Press, 1985).

Mattern, David B., et.al, eds., *The Papers of James Madison*, Volume 17: 31 March 1797–3 March 1801, with a supplement 22 January 1778–9 August 1795 (Chicago: The University of Chicago Press, 1991).

Machiavelli, Niccolo, *The Prince and the Discourses*, trans. by Luigi Ricci, revised by E.R.P. Vincent (New York: The Modern Library, 1950).

McDonald, Forrest, *Novus Ordo Seclorum: The Intellectual Origins of the Constitution* (Lawrence, Kansas: University Press of Kansas, 1985).

Montesquieu, Charles-Louis de Secondat, Baron de la Brede et de, *The Spirit of the Laws*, trans. and ed. by Anne M. Cohler, Basia Carolyn Miller, and Harold Samuel Stone (Cambridge: Cambridge University Press, 1989).

Munoz, Vincent Phillip, "James Madison's Principle of Religious Liberty," *The American Political Science Review* 97, No. 1 (2003): 17–32.

Pocock, J.G.A., *The Machiavellian Moment: Florentine Political Thought and the Atlantic Republican Tradition* (Princeton: Princeton University Press, 1975).

Polybius, *The Histories*, trans. by Robin Waterfield (Oxford: Oxford University Press, 2010).

Read, James H., *Power versus Liberty: Madison, Hamilton, Wilson, and Jefferson* (Charlottesville: University Press of Virginia, 2000).

Rosano, Michael J., "Liberty, Nobility, Philanthropy, and Power in Alexander Hamilton's Conception of Human Nature," *American Journal of Political Science* 47, No. 1 (2003): 61–74.

Rutland, Robert A., et. al, eds., *The Papers of James Madison*, Volume 8: 10 March 1784 – 28 March 1786 (Chicago: The University of Chicago Press, 1973).

Rutland, Robert A., et.al, eds., *The Papers of James Madison*, Volume 10: 27 May 1787–3 March 1788 (Chicago: The University of Chicago Press, 1977).

Rutland, Robert A., et.al, eds., *The Papers of James Madison*, Volume 11: 7 March 1788–1 March 1789 (Chicago: The University of Chicago Press, 1977).

Rutland, Robert A., et.al, eds., *The Papers of James Madison*, Volume 14: 6 April 1791–16 March 1793 (Chicago: The University of Chicago Press, 1983).

Schwarz, Michael, "The Great Divergence Reconsidered: Hamilton, Madison, and U.S.-British Relations, 1783–89," *Journal of the Early Republic* 27, no. 3 (2007): 407–436.

Sheehan, Colleen A., "Madison v. Hamilton: The Battle Over Republicanism and the Role of Public Opinion," *American Political Science Review* 98, no. 3 (2004): 405–424.

Sidney, Algernon, *Discourses Concerning Government*, ed. by Thomas G. West (Indianapolis: Liberty Classics, 1990).

Stagg, J. C. A., et.al, eds., *The Papers of James Madison*, Volume 16: 27 April 1795–27 March 1797 (Chicago: The University of Chicago Press, 1989).

Syrett, Harold C., ed., and Jacob E. Cooke, assoc. ed., *The Papers of Alexander Hamilton*, volume I: 1768–1778 (New York: Columbia University Press, 1961).

Syrett, Harold C., ed., and Jacob E. Cooke, assoc. ed., *The Papers of Alexander Hamilton*, volume II: 1779–1781 (New York: Columbia University Press, 1961).

Syrett, Harold C., ed., and Jacob E. Cooke, assoc. ed., *The Papers of Alexander Hamilton*, volume III: 1782–1786 (New York: Columbia University Press, 1962).

Syrett, Harold C., ed., and Jacob E. Cooke, assoc. ed., *The Papers of Alexander Hamilton*, volume V: June 1788–November 1789 (New York: Columbia University Press, 1962).

Syrett, Harold C., ed., and Jacob E. Cooke, assoc. ed., *The Papers of Alexander Hamilton*, volume VII: September 1790–January 1791 (New York: Columbia University Press, 1963).

Syrett, Harold C., ed., and Jacob E. Cooke, assoc. ed., *The Papers of Alexander Hamilton*, volume VIII: February 1791–July 1791 (New York: Columbia University Press, 1965).

Syrett, Harold C., ed., and Jacob E. Cooke, assoc. ed., *The Papers of Alexander Hamilton*, volume IX: August 1791–December 1791 (New York: Columbia University Press, 1965).

Syrett, Harold C., ed., and Jacob E. Cooke, assoc. ed., *The Papers of Alexander Hamilton*, volume X: December 1791 January 1792 (New York: Columbia University Press, 1966).

Syrett, Harold C., ed., and Jacob E. Cooke, assoc. ed., *The Papers of Alexander Hamilton*, volume XI: February 1792–June 1792 (New York: Columbia University Press, 1966).

Syrett, Harold C., ed., and Jacob E. Cooke, assoc. ed., *The Papers of Alexander Hamilton*, volume XII: July 1792–October 1792 (New York: Columbia University Press, 1967).

Syrett, Harold C., ed., and Jacob E. Cook, assoc. ed., *The Papers of Alexander Hamilton*, volume XIV: February 1793–June 1793 (New York: Columbia University Press, 1969).

Syrett, Harold C., ed., and Jacob E. Cooke, assoc. ed., *The Papers of Alexander Hamilton*, volume XVI: February 1794–July 1794 (New York: Columbia University Press, 1972).

Syrett, Harold C., ed., and Jacob E. Cooke, assoc. ed., *The Papers of Alexander Hamilton*, volume XVII: August 1794–December 1794 (New York: Columbia University Press, 1972).

Syrett, Harold C., ed., *The Papers of Alexander Hamilton*, volume XVIII: January 1795–July 1795 (New York: Columbia University Press, 1973).

Syrett, Harold C., ed., *The Papers of Alexander Hamilton*, volume XX: January 1796–March 1797 (New York: Columbia University Press, 1974).

Syrett, Harold C., ed., *The Papers of Alexander Hamilton*, volume XXI: April 1797–July 1798 (New York: Columbia University Press, 1974).

Syrett, Harold C., ed., *The Papers of Alexander Hamilton*, volume XXII: July 1798–March 1799 (New York: Columbia University Press, 1975).

Syrett, Harold C., ed., *The Papers of Alexander Hamilton*, volume XXIV: November 1799–June 1800 (New York: Columbia University Press, 1976).

Syrett, Harold C., ed., *The Papers of Alexander Hamilton*, volume XXV: July 1800–April 1802 (New York: Columbia University Press, 1977).

Syrett, Harold C., ed., *The Papers of Alexander Hamilton*, volume XXVI: May 1, 1802–October 23, 1804, Additional Documents 1774–1799, Addenda and Errata (New York: Columbia University Press, 1979).

Trenchard, John and Thomas Gordon, *Cato's Letters*, third edition (New York: Russell & Russell, 1969).

Index

About the Author

William J. Nichols is an instructor at Wayne County Community College in Detroit, Michigan. He has a BA in political science from the University of Iowa, an MA in political science from Marquette University, and a PhD from Wayne State University. Originally from Iowa, he now lives and works in Detroit, a place he never thought he would have ended up.

www.ingramcontent.com/pod-product-compliance
Ingram Content Group UK Ltd.
Pitfield, Milton Keynes, MK11 3LW, UK
UKHW041840031026
15587UKWH00002B/915

9 781793 655363